Driving Through Georgian Britain:

The great coaching routes for the modern traveller.

The Great North Road, the Bath Road, the Dover Road and the Road to Brighton.

by

Louise Allen

Contents

Introduction   6

Sources   9

Following the routes and eating at the inns   11

The Great North Road   12

London to North Finchley   13

North Finchley to Bell Bar   16

Bell Bar to Welwyn   19

Welwyn to Baldock   23

Baldock to Eaton Socon   26

Eaton Socon to Stilton   29

Stilton to Stamford   33

Stamford to Grantham   36

Grantham to Doncaster   38

Doncaster to York   45

York to Northallerton   49

Doncaster to Wetherby   51

Wetherby to Northallerton   56

Northallerton to Darlington   58

Darlington to Durham   61

Durham to Newcastle   64

Newcastle to Morpeth   66

Morpeth to the Border   70

The Border to Edinburgh   74

The Traveller Arrives In Edinburgh   79

The Dover Road   81

    Southwark to Deptford   82

    Deptford, Blackheath & Shooters Hill to Crayford   87

    Crayford to Greenhithe   93

    Greenhithe to Strood   96

    Rochester to Sittingbourne   101

    Sittingbourne to Canterbury   106

    Canterbury   110

    Gutteridge Gate to Dover   113

The Brighton Road   119

The 'Classic' Route from 1816   119

    Southwark to the Elephant and Castle   119

    Westminster Bridge Variation   120

    Elephant and Castle to Kennington   120

    Kennington to Streatham   122

    Streatham to Croydon   126

    Croydon to Merstham   129

    Merstham to Povey Cross   131

    Povey Cross to Hand Cross   133

    Hand Cross to Brighton   136

Sutton & Reigate Variation of the 'Classic' Route   140

    Kennington to Mitcham   140

    Mitcham to Reigate   142

    Reigate to Povey Cross   144

The Old Route used from the 17th century   144

    London to Blindley Heath   144

Blindley Heath to Forest Row   145

Forest Row to Uckfield   148

Uckfield to Brighton   149

The Bath Road   153

The Stage Coaches   155

Following the Bath Road Today   156

London to Kensington   157

Kensington to Hounslow   166

Hounslow to Slough   172

Slough to Reading   176

Reading to Speen   181

Speen to Beckhampton   188

Beckhampton to Chippenham   192

Chippenham to Bath   197

Index   201

About the Author   208

Introduction

The Georgian era was the highpoint of horse-powered travel. Roads were improving out of all recognition, the network of inns across the country provided travellers with fresh horses, food and shelter while road books and maps sent them accurately on their way. Stage and Mail coaches criss-crossed the country cutting journey times from weeks to days, or even hours compared with previous centuries.

Then, in the 1840s, the railways came and an entire industry was changed for ever, prosperous little towns declined into villages, bustling villages became hamlets and the state of the roads themselves declined until the arrival of the bicycle and the motorcar revived long-distance road travel.

The memory of coaching days lingered on into the Victorian period with the romantic glow of past times – jolly landlords, keen-eyed drivers, dashing highwaymen, the guard with his yard of tin, Regency bucks with their curricles and phaetons... The names of the old routes still conjure up those images: The Bath Road, the Brighton Road, the Dover Road and the Great North Road.

I began to trace these old routes as research for historical novels, then found they were fascinating to drive today. This book is for my fellow historical novelists, but also for anyone who wants to turn a journey into an excursion, who prefers to take country roads as a relief from motorways, to find old inns instead of service stations and to admire villages and historic towns instead of by-passing them.

On my explorations I found two fellow passengers from the past whose company brought the old roads to life. Colonel John Byng, later Viscount Torrington (1743-1813), was an enthusiast traveller, mostly on horseback. He was an early tourist, travelling for pleasure, and made at least fourteen extended journeys around England and Wales, never hesitating to record what he thought. He was no sufferer of fools, nor did he mince his words when he encountered a substandard inn. His *Rides Round Britain* is still available if you can find a copy of the excellent Folio Society edition (1996).

Another outspoken traveller was Charles G. Harper (1863-1943) He was a keen cyclist who was exploring the great roads at a time when the stories of coaching days were still being told by those who had lived through them. Harper was fascinated by coaching days and his 'Road' books, and books on old inns, are a constant entertainment and source of information. He too did not hesitate to speak his mind – he was vehemently against motor cars, disliked modern industry and held a deep prejudice against various noblemen. I quote him, but needless to say, his opinions are his own.

In this book I have concentrated on tracing the old routes amidst the modern traffic and trying to find the buildings and landmarks the Georgian traveller would have seen. It does not attempt to replace guidebooks to individual places – there are far too many for that – instead I hope it will help you to do your own detective work, finding the remnants and ghosts of another age.

Sources

Charles G. Harper's and John Byng's books are mentioned above. *The Directory of Stage Coach Services 1836* by Alan Bates (David & Charles 1969) gives the timetables for the stage and mail and the inns where they started and finished their journey at the peak of coach travel.

Celia Fiennes (1162-1741) was helpful for the Dover Road – various editions of her diaries are available.

Pierce Egan: Walks Through Bath (1819) is quoted in the Bath Road section.

For an insight into the experiences of the mail and stage coach traveller in terms of comfort, safely and refreshment along the way there is my *Travel By Stagecoach* (Shire 2014).

For maps I have used the Cassini Historical editions of the Old Series Ordnance Survey One-inch maps (not available for Scotland) and various maps published by John Cary in the late 18th and early 19th century, particularly *Cary's New Map of England and Wales with Part of Scotland on which are carefully laid down All the Direct and Principal Cross Roads...* This was published as an atlas in 1794.

The London Topographical Society's *A-Z of Regency London* and *A-Z of Georgian London* are invaluable for tracing routes out of London and *The Village London Atlas: the changing face of Greater London 1822-1903* (Alderman Press 1986) extends northwards to St Albans and Hoddesdon, eastward to Dartford, south to Reigate and west to Windsor.

Various original road books were used, principally *Cary's New Itinerary; or, An accurate delineation of the great roads both direct and cross throughout England and Wales: with many of the principal roads in Scotland* (1812 edition), *Paterson's Roads* by Edward Mogg (18th edition 1826), *Owen's New Book of Roads* (1805) and Gray's *New Book of Roads: The Tourist and Traveller's Guide to the Roads* (1824)

Following the Routes & Eating
At the Inns

Each section of the route begins with instructions on tracing it on modern roads, followed by a description of that section as the Georgian traveller would have experienced it. Most of the roads and lanes can also be followed by the armchair traveller on StreetView.

Numerous inns are mentioned, many of which are still in existence. The opinion of earlier travellers should not, of course, be taken as any indication of their character now, nor have I attempted to assess them for their modern standards of hospitality.

The Great North Road

If you want to travel between London to Edinburgh today you can drive the four hundred miles in about eight hours, take the train in approximately four and a half hours or fly in an hour. Three hundred years ago you would make your will and brace yourself for several weeks of dangerous, slow, uncomfortable travel.

By the early years of the 19th century you could have made the journey by stage or mail coach, or hired a post chaise, and it could have taken you as little as forty hours.

The road you would have taken was the Great North Road, perhaps the most famous and romantic of the great coaching routes. There is both an Old North Road and a Great North Road. The Old North Road, following the Roman Ermine Street, runs through Waltham Cross, Ware, Royston and Huntingdon. The Great North Road leaves London from Smithfield and passes through Barnet, Hatfield and Biggleswade before they meet at Alconbury. We will follow the Great North Road.

The very wealthy who travelled in their own private coach, or those hiring a post chaise, another expensive option, at least had the luxury of setting their own pace, choosing their inns and packing their own bed linen to combat fleas and bedbugs. At the other end of the social scale, travellers used the lumbering stage wagons, rode or even walked.

Distances are in miles as measured from Hick's Hall. Great North Road has been abbreviated to GNR in most places.

London to North Finchley

Start in Smithfield, pass through the Victorian market buildings to St John's Street (B501). Go north to A1 to Highbury Corner then take the Holloway Road to the roundabout at Archway Underground station. Take the B519 through Highgate Village and right onto North Road, becoming North Hill, to A1000. Continue north to North Finchley.

*

The Great North Road starts in Smithfield where St John's Street winds north from the great Victorian market buildings. They transformed the historic open space that saw heretics burned at the stake in Tudor times. The Georgian traveller would recognise the entrance into the churchyard of St Bartholomew the Great and also the Henry VIII entrance into Bart's (St Bartholomew's Hospital) founded in 1123 and still on the same site, but little else remains of what used to be a huge lozenge-shaped open market.

St John's Lane comes in from the west a short distance along St John's Street from the junction with Charterhouse Street. The road widens here and this was the site of Hick's Hall, constructed in 1611 as the first purpose-built sessions house for magistrates. Traditionally distances on the GNR were measured from the front of the building and that location was still used, even after it was demolished in 1778.

The stage or mail coach traveller would have begun their journey further south in the City of London at, for example, *The George and Blue Boar* in Holborn, *The Saracen's Head* in Snow Hill, *The White Horse* in Fetter Lane or *The Belle Sauvage* on

Ludgate Hill. If they were taking a Mail coach they might well have chosen *The Bull and Mouth* close to the General Post Office in St Martin le Grand. The Mail left *The Bull and Mouth* at 7.30 in the evening, stopped to load the mails at the General Post Office and were away by 8pm.

The first mile takes us to Islington, then a village just on the edge of London. Even so close to the City, the road was a dangerous one, infested with footpads, and the coach passengers would have been glad of their team of fresh horses and their armed guard. Just after the modern junction with the A502 we pass some buildings of the City University on the right, more or less opposite the location of the first turnpike gate out of London.

On the left was the reservoir of the New River Head, Sadler's Wells theatre and a tea garden for excursions out of London. There have been six theatres here dating back to 1683 and in 1801 both the young Edmund Kean and Grimaldi the clown appeared there.

Across the City Road is the village of Islington (*1¼ miles*). There are still the remains of the large village green, once fringed with elm trees and with its own, very minor, mineral springs. The village was popular with City shopkeepers and merchants as somewhere respectable to retire to and it was the location of a number of coaching inns: *The Peacock*, the Elizabethan *Queen's Head* and *The Angel*, the name of which lives on in a Victorian pub and the Underground station.

The route continues out of Islington and turns to the north west, continually climbing towards Highgate. What is now

Holloway Road was then The Hollow Way, an ancient track between steep banks, infested with footpads and highwaymen and mired in mud whenever it rained. There were very few houses, even by the 1820s.

At the roundabout by Archway underground station, the location of *The Archway Tavern* (*4¼ miles*), the road forks left onto Highgate Hill. This was the original route before Archway Road was cut through the hill itself. Tunnels had been tried, but all collapsed and eventually John Rennie drove an open cutting through. It was bridged in 1813 and the current bridge dates from 1897. Coaches could then take the much easier gradient to Finchley, although anyone wanting to avoid the gate, and its very high tolls, would still take the old route through Highgate Village, as we will.

A short distance up Highgate Hill, on the left just past the modern *Whittington Stone* pub, is the Stone itself. This commemorates Dick Whittington, three times Lord Mayor of London, who legend says, was discouraged by his lack of success and was leaving London with his cat when he heard the sound of the bells calling, 'Turn again, Whittington…' The present stone in an iron cage has the cat on top and dates from 1821, although the cage is later and the lettering has been recut.

The hill beyond is very steep and was another location favoured by footpads. The great clown Joseph Grimaldi was set upon here in 1807, but he was recognised by his admiring assailants and released with his watch and money intact. Highgate, 400 feet above sea level, still has a definite village atmosphere, but it retains none of its original coaching inns and the toll gate has long disappeared. At the end of the High Street the road turns right downhill to East Finchley.

In the 19th century what is now the crossroads with the A1/Holloway Road was the location of the charmingly-named *Dirt House*, actually *The White Lion* inn. (The present *Old White Lion* does not appear to be on the same site). The name is said to derive from it being a stopping place for the market wagons taking produce into London and then returning with loads of dirt and manure for the local farms.

East Finchley was simply a hamlet of scattered cottages and most of the area was taken up by the wild expanse of Finchley Common (*7 miles*), known in the 18th century as one of the most dangerous places in the country for highwaymen, including Dick Turpin. The so-called Turpin's Oak tree was on the left, just before the road reaches the modern North Circular Road and was said to be peppered with musket balls. The notorious criminal Jack Shepherd was caught on the Common in 1724 after his fifth, and final, breakout from Newgate prison. He was hanged in November at Tyburn. The enclosure of the common for farming began in 1816 and put an end to these dangers.

In North Finchley is Tally Ho Corner named for the 'Tally Ho' coaching company that, in the 1820s, kept a large stables here to change horses for the final run into London.

North Finchley to Bell Bar

A1000 through Whetstone, Chipping Barnet, Hadley Green, Potters Bar and Bell Bar.

The next village was Whetstone (*9¼ miles*), said to derive its name from the old stone in front of *The Griffin* public house, reputedly where soldiers 'whetted' the edge of their weapons before the Battle of Barnet (1471). Unfortunately, the stone is probably just the base of the old inn sign or even a mounting block. It can still be seen in the pavement in front of the pub, close to the corner with the A109 in the centre of the old community.

Whetstone was a straggling farming village in coaching days and Chaplin, one of the major coaching proprietors, maintained dozens of horses here for the first change out of London. A further mile and a half north was Whetstone Gate, a sight welcomed by regular travellers who knew that they were now clear of the dangers of Finchley Common. In 1834 ninety coaches passed through the gate every twenty four hours. Pickfords, still a removal company today, ran a network of carts and wagons and grazed two hundred horses at Whetstone.

The road across Finchley Common and on to Barnet was notoriously bad, as well as rising very steeply up Prickler's Hill towards Chipping Barnet. In 1810 the Whetstone and Highgate Turnpike Trust remade the eight mile stretch and it was considered to be amongst the best roads in the country. However, in 1823 there was an Act for the improvement of the road from London to Holyhead and the surveyors insisted that the gradient was reduced further. Telford and McAdam came up with rival schemes and eventually McAdam's was adopted and the worst of the dip was filled in and embanked between 1823-7. To the left on the road north into Chipping Barnet the houses are low down on the original line, showing what an exceedingly steep climb it must originally have been.

Chipping Barnet (*11¼ miles*) stands on a high ridge running west-east. For most coach proprietors it was the first stop after London and, as the Great North Road and the Holyhead Road divide just north of the town, it was very prosperous – at least until 1838 when the railway arrived.

Coaches for Stamford, York, Shrewsbury, Birmingham, Manchester and Liverpool would all stop here and, for passengers from London, this was the first opportunity for refreshments. It was also exceedingly busy with changes for post chaises. There was fierce rivalry between the inns which were local political centres, as well as being commercial rivals. *The Red Lion* was Tory, *The Green Man* was Whig. Neither survives and the A1081 now cuts through the site of *The Red Lion's* stable yard.

Hadley Green comes almost immediately after Chipping Barnet. It retains some handsome old houses and the Hadley High Stone (*12 miles*). This obelisk was erected in 1740 on the spot where the Earl of Warwick is said to have been killed at the Battle of Barnet (April 14th 1471) when he was defeated by Edward IV, marking the end of the Lancastrian cause. The minor road that forks off to the left here is the original Holyhead road.

Now on high ground, the GNR is level as it passes Wrotham Park to the left. 'Near 250 acres form the attached park, which receives a considerable degree of natural beauty from the fine natural slopes and the abundance of wood.' (*Paterson's Roads.*) At the hamlet of Ganwick Corner *The Duke of York* inn still looks much as it did when it was built in 1745. Originally *The White Horse,* it was renamed in 1800. There is an old milestone reading 'London 13 Miles' just outside.

The road cuts across what was open farmland and heath before reaching Potter's Bar (*14¼ miles*). Before the railway arrived, Potters Bar was a straggling village along the line of the Great North Road with none of the commuter development that now fills the valley to the east, around the railway station. At the northern end, where the road to Northaw forks off to the left, was the tollgate, although it was not this that gave the village its name. In the 13th century the land was owned by Geoffrey de Pottere who gated, or barred, his boundaries: hence Potter's Bar.

Two miles along the undulating road is the left turning to Mymms. This is approximately where the old road continued due north along the eastern boundaries of Gobions and then Brookmans Park. That route cannot be followed now because of modern developments, but the main road continues on a cutting driven through in 1822 to smooth out the route.

Bell Bar to Welwyn

Turn left into Bell Lane. Continue through to A1000, cross into Woodside Lane. Left into Wildhill Road. Return to A1000 and turn right to Old Hatfield onto Broadway and right into Fore Street. Return to A1000, follow signs for Hertford, then left onto A414. At Junction 4 roundabout with A1(M) take A6129, then left at first roundabout. B653, right into Lemsford Lane to Lemsford village. Under the A1(M) and left onto B197. First left into Ayot Green, then return to B197 to Old Welwyn. Left on London Road to High Street.

*

The old route can be picked up by turning into Bell Lane. This narrow lane turns north in two sharp bends and at the second of those becomes the Great North Road, with a remnant remaining to the south where it now runs into a farmyard. This tiny hamlet with a few 18th century houses is all that remains of Bell Bar (*17¼ miles*). The road can be followed through back to the 'new' road with the old *Swan Inn*, now a private dwelling, on the left.

The original route went straight ahead, across the A1000, into the trees. The road forks after half a mile and the Great North Road took the left fork, now cut off. To see where it went through Hatfield Park, continue to Wildhill Road, turn left and a few yards further on to the right there are gates to a driveway. This is the ancient route through the Park to the gates of the house itself. Eventually, in the early 18th century, Lord Salisbury had the new road made to skirt his property as far as Old Hatfield (*19¾ miles*).

In Old Hatfield the right turn into Fore Street leads up to the gates of Hatfield House. The old Great North Road would have come in from the park to the right and turned down the steep and narrow Fore Street before turning sharply right between *The Four Bells* inn, which still remains, and *The Chequers* on the other side of the road.

Modern changes to the road pattern mean that it is necessary to return to the main road, turn in the direction of Hertford and continue past the large, 18th century, *Red Lion Inn* on the right.

This would have served the busy crossroads of the Great North Road and the Hertford road.

At the traffic lights go straight across. This small street leads to the railway and, at this point, the magnificent Great North Road dwindles to a footbridge over the tracks. The road remains on the far side and emerges just before Junction 4 of the A1(M) where the route has been obliterated from here to Stanborough.

At Stanborough (*21½ miles*) there is a small stub of the Great North Road at the first roundabout after passing under the A1(M). There is not much left of what Harper calls 'the tree-shaded hamlet' of Stanborough, but there is a choice of routes here. The newer road is the fourth exit from the roundabout and runs alongside the motorway into Lemsford. It is flat and dull, so to experience the route as it would have been in the 18th and early nineteenth centuries, take the B653 up the hill for two miles. As the road begins to level out it reaches the corner of Brocket Park surrounding, 'The magnificent seat of Lord Viscount Melbourne.' (*Paterson's Roads*).

The old route turns right into Lemsford Road and, following the brick wall of the park, plunges down into the valley of the little River Lea and Lemsford village. (*22¼ miles*)

The stagecoach passengers would have seen water meadows, mills and, just before they cross the brick bridge, *The Sun*, a small local alehouse which is still there. On the other side of the bridge, just to the left of the modern *Long And Short Arm* pub, the road turned left, hugging the park wall, and continued north. Its ghost, vanishing into scrub, can just be glimpsed through the fence in the pub car park.

To find the GNR again, go under the motorway and then turn onto the B197 which parallels the main road, then cross the motorway into Ayot Green, a tiny village around a large green at the summit of Digswell Hill. Take the left turn immediately after crossing the bridge and you are back on the GNR, although the road ends just after *The Waggoner's*, an old inn that must have seen considerable traffic in the old days.

The B197 after the Ayot Green turn returns to the line of the GNR. It passes the old *Red Lion* inn on the left before beginning the long and curving descent of Digswell Hill (*23¼ miles*). Carefully braking must have been necessary as it is downhill for almost two miles into the valley of the little River Mimram, a shallow stream running over a pebbly bottom through water meadows.

The road enters the modern outskirts of Welwyn village and turns down London Road. This was still open country when the coaches ran and the passengers on top of the coach would not have seen the village (*25¼ miles*) until the road took an abrupt plunge down the hill. Ahead is *The White Hart*, one of the two large coaching inns in the village, with its stable yard arch facing directly up the hill. It kept the horses for the *Stamford Flyer*. Further into the village, when the London Road has become the High Street and reached the church, is *The Wellington*, the second coaching inn. Welwyn retains many old red-brick buildings and it is easy to imagine the coaches passing through here.

Colonel Byng (see Introduction), stayed at *The White Hart*

on 26th May 1792, immediately after a very unpleasant night at its namesake in St Albans. He was on a tour into the North up the Great North Road having joined it, 'at the twenty-second milestone.'

'The White Hart appear'd magnificent after that of St Albans,' he wrote. 'I prowled about the pretty environs of this village until half-past eight o'clock, when I was summon'd to eat of an eel, etc.' In his account he notes the cost of his stay: eel 1s 6d, bread and cheese 2d, brandy 1s, wine 1s 3d, paper 1d, rushlight 2d and breakfast 10d: a total of 5 shillings. He does not mention stabling costs for his horse, a chestnut mare named Spot. He had already sent his other horse, Bumper, a bay gelding, ahead to Biggleswade where he would meet his valet Garwood.

Welwyn to Baldock

Take Codicote Road to left of church then turn right onto B656. Across roundabout to B197 through Knebworth to Stevenage. Turn left onto London Road and continue to Six Hills Roundabout. Join A602. Turn right at second roundabout to Trinity Road, then left into Stevenage Old Town High Street. Leave on A602 then B197 to Graveley. A505 then B197, following signs for Baldock.

*

The GNR turned sharply right to pass in front of Welwyn church, but modern through traffic must take the bypass to the A1(M) roundabout. The Great North Road goes under the motorway again and climbs a long hill. It is lined with houses now, but the coaches would have passed through farmland and across Mardley Heath, an area of gorse and woodland with good views over the Mimram valley, before reaching the hilltop and the hamlet of Woolmer Green (*27¼ miles*). Originally the road ran on through farmland until it began the long descent into Broadwater, but now the commuter village of Knebworth, formed after the railway arrived, occupies the whole crest of the hill.

The hill begins to descend towards Stevenage through open farmland with the valley of the Stevenage Brook to the east. Broadwater (*29½ miles*), where there is now a roundabout at the foot of the hill, was a tiny hamlet, two miles from the small market town of Stevenage.

Continuing northwards along London Road the road passes, '...six large barrows lying in a row. These are generally supposed to be of Danish origin.' (*Paterson's Roads.*) They are actually prehistoric burial mounds, known as the Six Hills. It was a standard joke amongst coach drivers to bet with passengers which two were the furthest apart – the first and the last, obviously, but it seems to have regularly baffled passengers and won the drivers a number of bumpers of brandy. Readers of Georgette Heyer's *The Foundling* will recognise the joke, as this is the route the Duke of Sale takes by stagecoach when he sets out to have an adventure.

The GNR is lost under the new town from this point. Continuing north, Stevenage Old Town's High Street lies to the east of the modern road. 'Stevenage... consists of one large and several smaller streets, the houses of which are, however, indifferently built.' (*Paterson's Roads*)

The High Street (*31½ miles*) is wide, marking this out as both a market town and one that needed room for stage and Mail coaches. Its most famous 'inhabitant' is probably Henry Trigg who was so afraid of body snatchers that he insisted in his will that his coffin was placed in the rafters of a barn. He died in 1724 and the coffin remained there when the barn became *The Old Castle Inn* in 1774. In 1999 the inn became a bank and the company insisted the body was buried in the churchyard, although the coffin is still there. (NatWest Bank, 37, High Street). *The White Swan* was the main source of post horses.

Graveley (*33½ miles*), the next settlement, is a charming little village that would probably still be recognisable to the coach passengers. They may have stopped for refreshment at *The George and Dragon*, next to the humbler ale house of *The Wagon and Horses*.

The road rises gently through Graveley and runs northwards across open, undulating, farmland before descending the long hill down into the head of the Ivel valley and the market town of Baldock (*37½ miles*). The town has an extensive, wide, high street lined with handsome 18th century houses and inns and the numerous eating places testify to the fact that it is still an important rest stop for travellers.

The White Horse supplied horses for post chaises. This inn was a focal point for action in Heyer's *The Foundling* and still stands at the junction where the GNR takes a sharp right-left turn out of the town and the road to Newmarket and Cambridge continues off to the east. Originally its yards and stables extended over the whole area of the car park. It was here, where the toll gate stood, that highwaymen took £500 in coin from the Newcastle stage wagon in 1737.

Baldock to Eaton Socon

Leave Baldock on the A507 (Station Road, then North Road) then A1 north. At first roundabout take A6001 (London Road) through Biggleswade to rejoin the A1. Just past Beeston take slip road signed Bedford (A603). Turn right and right again to cross Girtford Bridge. Rejoin A1. Turn off for Eaton Socon (A428, signposted Cambridge) and then the B1428, then B1041 through the town to the A1.

*

To your left as the road leaves Baldock are three old water mills, then the old road vanishes under the A1 North as it crosses the county boundary out of Hertfordshire into Bedfordshire. It runs downhill into the valley of the tiny Cat Ditch brook, and past a half-timbered building on the left, now *The Tudor Oaks Lodge* and originally *The New Inn* and the location of a turnpike gate (*40¼ miles*).

From the Cat Ditch the road begins the long haul up Topler's Hill, crowned by a 20th century water tower. The fields on either side are dotted with farms and small villages and now, as then, produce vegetables for the London market.

The old route leaves the A1 and the bypass to enter Biggleswade (*45¼ miles*) where the square in the centre testifies to the importance of the market here and how busy it was with stage and mail coaches. Two inns, *The Crown* and *The White Swan* faced each other across the narrow street at the exit of the market square. Now only *The Crown* remains with its arched entrance to the stable yard and the legend '1785. Horses & Carriages for hire. Livery & bait stables'. The centre of the town around the market square was destroyed in a fire in June 1785.

The White Swan horsed the *Regent* coach and at one time the landlord was a miserable man called Crouch who kept the place freezing cold. Only twenty minutes were allowed for the refreshment stops and travellers report emerging colder and more hungry than they had gone in.

The road turns right just after *The Crown* and the buildings to the left all back onto the River Ivel. Up until the mid-19th century Biggleswade was the head of navigation for the river and old wharves for coal and timber line the banks. On the right one handsome three storey red-brick Georgian house still bears the inscription 'Establishment for Young Gentlemen' across the front.

Sun Street comes in from the right just before the river crossing is reached. This road bypasses the market square and was the location of *The Sun Inn*, now a private house. In its day it had twenty four bed chambers and kept forty four horses, six post-chaises and two carriages for hire. One of the original mounting blocks can still be seen in front of the building.

This was the inn patronised by Colonel Byng (later Lord Torrington and not Lord Terrington as the plaque on the building says).

He arrived there at half-past eleven having ridden from Welwyn. 'I had for my dinner at two o'clock (the hour of rational and useful appetite) a boil'd fowl, greens, roast beef, Yorkshire pudding, asparagus, tarts and custards! When I ate like a parson or a farmer (Swift could not decide who was the better eater), and so greedily at first that I only eyed and threaten'd the tarts and custards.' After the arrival of his valet and a two mile walk before tea he retired to bed, 'to sheets my own', at eleven o'clock.

Byng stayed until 29th May, encountering while he was in Biggleswade the famous landscape gardener, Humphrey Repton who was an old, and apparently very opinionated, acquaintance. The bill at *The Sun* was sixteen shillings: 'Nowhere shall I find a cheaper charge.'

The GNR crosses the River Ivel and continues on the A1 north. The valley of the Ivel here was very prone to flooding and the road through the hamlets of Lower Caldecote, Seddington and Beeston Green (*48¼ miles*) was often mired and difficult. Just past Beeston the GNR survives as a slip road signposted Bedford (A603). This leads to handsome Girtford Bridge, built in 1783 of local ironstone.

The GNR turned left immediately after crossing the bridge and ran into Girtford (*49¼ miles*) on the other side of the A1. Girtford is now absorbed into the market town of Sandy but it is possible to cross the A1 at the roundabout and find the remains of the old village street the coaches would have passed along.

Traffic continued along the route of the A1 across low-lying, rich, but waterlogged agricultural land. Just before the village of Tempsford (*51 miles*) the River Ivel joins the Great Ouse, greatly increasing the risk of flooding. The river was crossed, just north of Tempsford, by a narrow medieval bridge. Work started on its replacement in 1814 and took six years to complete. It is this new bridge that carries the northbound side of the road and the southbound crosses on a modern bridge.

Some coaches, including *The Regent*, would branch off to St Neots just before Tempsford bridge and risk the low-lying route to Huntingdon, but there are records of coaches on that road being so awash that the passengers had to perch crouching on the seats to keep out of the water.

It was safer to continue through Eaton Socon (*55¼ miles*) on the slightly higher western bank where the river makes a great loop just before the town. We can follow the GNR through the town which was always a straggling place, once important enough in the Middle Ages for a castle. Dickens stayed at *The White Horse* and called the place Eaton Slocombe, an indication of how it had declined. The other principal inn was *The Cock*.

The road rises, following a ridge where a windmill stands on top of the hill in open fields, marking the end of the village. The mill can still be seen on the left, just past the Co-Op supermarket. At the end of the ridge the GNR rejoins the A1 as it drops down to the valley of the little River Kym where the Ram Inn once stood.

Eaton Socon to Stilton

A1 to Buckden. At the roundabout turn right into the village High Street. Rejoin A1, northbound. Turn off for Alconbury onto Great North Road, becoming Vinegar Hill. Cross A1, left onto Alconbury Hill, right onto B1043. Cross A1 following signs to Stilton, into Stilton village centre.

*

The GNR by-passed the tiny settlement of Little Paxton with

its paper mills and dipped down to cross deep Diddington Brook (*60 miles*) by a white-painted timber bridge in 'a pretty hollow', according to Harper. Now the A1 sweeps across and the tiny gorge can only be glimpsed in passing.

Buckden (*61¼ miles*), still has the remains of the 15th century red-brick palace of the Bishops of Lincoln which was regularly visited by royalty on their way up and down the GNR. Henry III stayed there in 1248, Edward I in 1291 and Richard III in 1483. Catherine of Aragon lived there briefly in 1533 after the annulment of her marriage to Henry VIII before being moved to Kimbolton Castle and Henry himself stayed there in 1541 with Catherine Howard, his fifth wife.

Buckden was an important coaching village as can be seen by the size of *The George* inn with its dozens of rooms and the remains of a large stableyard. Cartwright, the landlord at one time, would personally drive the York *Express* between Buckden and Welwyn daily – a distance of about 70 miles – and like many inn keepers and coachmen, he provided horses for several stages.

There were also *The Lion*, dating back to the 15th century and extended in the 18th century, *The Vine* which was rebuilt in the 18th century to extend its stables and *The Spread Eagle*, built in the 17th century and also upgraded in the 18th century.

In 1839 there were six express coaches daily in each direction between York (and Edinburgh), Leeds, Lincoln and Boston and London. The impact of the railways on the business of the village just a few years later is easy to imagine.

From Buckden the GNR ran to the west of Godmanchester

and Huntingdon through open farmland, passing Brampton which lies between the road and Godmanchester. The village was probably the birthplace of Samuel Pepys and it was here, when a Dutch invasion was feared, that he fled from London and buried £1,300 in the garden of his parents' house.

The A1 now crosses the A14 where the *Brampton Hut* inn (*63¾ miles*) used to stand. It was obviously well-used for it was rebuilt several times and the junction is still known as Brampton Hut.

About a mile north of *Brampton Hut* was the scene of one of the gruesome murders with which stagecoach drivers and guards liked to entertain their passengers. Alconbury Brook curves close to the road at the point where now a southbound slip road brings traffic from an industrial estate onto the A1. This was the site of Matcham's Bridge where, in 1780, Gervase Matcham, a colourful character, murdered Benjamin Jones, a sixteen year old drummer boy, for the £7 they had been sent to collect by a certain Major Reynolds.

Matcham cut the lad's throat and escaped to serve in the navy. He had an attack of conscience during a thunderstorm in 1786, confessed and was executed at Huntingdon. His body was hanged in chains on Alconbury Hill, just to the north.

The GNR leaves the modern road to pass through Alconbury (*66¼ miles*) and up the long slope of Alconbury Hill (*68 miles*) where Matcham's body was placed in the gibbet. Here was a major junction where the Old North Road, the Roman Ermine Street, comes in from the south-east and the two routes join.

There is still an impressive monument to this junction, a large milestone which can now be found just after the turn onto the B1043, opposite a bus stop outside the industrial estate.

Nearby was *The Wheatsheaf* inn. It was not only a coaching inn, but also sent out more than thirty pairs of post-horses every day. Its business was ruined by the railways and it survived as a private house until the A1 improvements carried it away.

John Byng stayed there in 1792. 'Alconbury Inn is not calculated for windy weather, for wind searches every corner thereof… I had a large fire, for it is a bleak spot, and a good supper in a good room. I was… highly gratified with my bed, which was excellent, with a thick, smooth mattress… and curtains pleated like a paper lantern.'

The road drops down Stangate Hill to run along the edge of the hills. There was an expanse of fenland to the east, now drained, with the open water of Whittlesea Mere at its centre.

The road passes between the village of Sawtry All Saints and the hamlet of Sawtry St Judith on the right and, easily missed, the faint traces of the church of Sawtry St Andrew (*71½ miles*) on the right. Just north of the road across the A1 to Sawtry is a turning to the right to the modern cemetery (not signposted). In front of this is a copse of trees covering the site of the church and its graveyard. It is worth stopping to look, if only for the moving gravestone to James Ratford, killed in a duel in 1756.

Three miles on from the graveyard, just after the right turn to Connington, is a very large, two-winged farmhouse, mainly of red brick. This was once *The Crown and Woolpack* with large stables at the back for its posting and stagecoach business.

The GNR originally went straight on and into Stilton High Street (*75½ miles*). Now modern road changes mean it must be approached from the north.

This was one of the major coaching stops with the stage and mail coaches, post chaises and stage wagons mingling with great herds of animals being driven down to Smithfield. The two famous inns face each other across the wide street, the older, 17th century *Bell* on the east and *The Angel* (now an Indian restaurant) to the west.

The vast inn sign of *The Bell* is famous and it was here that Stilton cheese was first sold. 'Stilton has long been celebrated for the excellence of its cheese, which not unfrequently has been called the English Parmesan. It is asserted that this article was first made by Mrs Paulet of Wymondham, near Melton Mowbray, in Leicestershire, who supplied the celebrated Cooper Thornhill, who kept the Bell Inn in this village, with this new manufacture, which he often sold for 2s 6d per pound; and hence it is said to have first received its name from the place of sale.' (*Paterson's Roads.*) Thornhill was soon copied by the landlady of *The Angel*, Miss Worthington.

Stilton to Stamford

Drive north through Stilton on North Street (B1043). At the roundabout cross the A1 on the A15. Take first left into New Road and then immediately right for the Norman Cross monument. Retrace route to take A1 north. Take A6118 to Wansford. Turn right onto Bridge End. Cross bridge and continue up hill on A6118 to rejoin A1. Turn off on slip road signposted Stamford (B1081) London Road to town centre.

*

Just north of Stilton was the vast Norman Cross camp that held French prisoners during the Napoleonic wars (*76 miles*). It was begun in 1796 and held, on average, 5,500 prisoners at any one time. The camp was demolished in 1816. Trusted prisoners were let out on parole during the day, but if found after dark were liable to be shot at. Stage and mail coach guards taking potshots at suspicious characters winged several harmless locals until parole was stopped. The modern memorial with the brass eagle commemorates the 1,700 prisoners who died here in the camp that occupied the large field just to the north.

At the junction of what are now the A1 and the A605, the Peterborough road, was *Kate's Cabin* (*79¼*), an inn much frequented by travellers, but now vanished under the widened road. Just north of *Kate's Cabin*, and 79½ miles north of London, the road bends to the left. Ermine Street carried straight on here into the Roman garrison town of Durobrivae which lies tight against the northern edge of the road.

The road is now in the valley of the Nene and passes the hamlets of Water Newton (*81¼ miles*) and Sibson before entering Wansford (*84 miles*). The old village was on the far side of the Nene, in the county of Northamptonshire, and the great *Haycock Inn* at the bridge is in Huntingdonshire and, technically, in the village of Stibbington.

The Haycock is an inn again now, after a period following

34

the collapse of the coaching traffic when it became a private house. As well as being a coaching inn it provided accommodation for those coming to follow the Fitzwilliam hunt and could stable one hundred and fifty horses. It is still possible to get an idea of how busy the place was by looking round what remains of the yards and stables. John Byng '...found good accommodation and reception there as formerly.'

The bridge itself is ancient, dating back to 1577 and repaired and altered a number of times. It was a dangerous spot for coaches from the north, for the hill down to it is steep, has a tight curve and is crossed by the village street. Even from the south, drivers had to be skilled to get their team right before tackling the hill.

The GNR enters Stamford along the western edge of Burghley Park surrounding the great house built in the 16th century by William Cecil. As the road sweeps down into the valley of the Welland there is a handsome pair of lodges and gates on the right, exactly 89 miles from London. The town of Stamford (*89½ miles*) is beautifully preserved, with the High Street lined with stone-built houses from the 16th century onwards.

Many travellers would have stayed for several days at Stamford, to see the sights or attend the races. *The George Inn*, just before the bridge, was a notable landmark and the place to stay for any notables who were not accommodated at Burghley House. Charles I slept there in 1645 and the Duke of Cumberland, returning from the battle of Culloden, celebrated here with his officers. Coach passengers would also hear all about Daniel Lambert, the fattest man in England, who weighed almost fifty three stone and who died at Stamford in 1809.

Stamford to Grantham

Cross the river and leave Stamford on B1081 through Great Casterton to A1. Continue north on A1 to B6403 to Colsterworth, go through the village and rejoin A1. Take B1174 into Grantham.

*

The GNR rises steeply out of Stamford onto a level road with fine views as it enters Rutland and then descends to Great, or Bridge, Casterton (*91½ miles*) where the River Wash or Guash, is crossed. About a mile north of the junction where the route rejoins the A1 a large farm stands on the right-hand side in the middle of empty fields. Opposite this, on the GNR, was Bowlands' Gibbet where the body of highwayman John Bowland was exhibited in 1769. A short distance beyond this the large patch of woodland on the left is Bloody Oaks where the battle of Erpingham was fought in 1470, another source of lurid tales for passengers.

The road bends to the right to follow a more northerly direction, and on the left, difficult to spot behind hedges, is the old *Greetham Inn*, now a private house. It is marked on all the old maps as *The Oak* and there is apparently an inscription under the eaves reading 'This is the New Inn, 1786', but it was always known to the coachmen and postboys as the *Greetham Inn* (*97½ miles*).

John Byng refers to it as *The Royal Oak*. In 1792 he reports parlour, supper and wine as all being unpleasant. The bed (made up with his own sheets) was, however, satisfactory.

Daily as many as forty-four coaches, half going north, half

south, would change horses here and at *The Black Bull* a little further north. That means that between them there was a turnover of 176 horses every twenty four hours.

About a mile further north, just to the side of the petrol station, is *The Ram Jam Inn* (*97¼ miles*). This was originally a local beer house called *The Winchilsea Arms*, but it seems to have acquired its odd name in the 1740s when the new landlord, an officer's servant, returned from India and introduced a mysterious liqueur he called Ram Jan.

Its other claim to fame was as the lodgings for Molyneux, the black bare-knuckle fighter, on the night before he met Tom Cribb at Thistleton Gap nearby on 28th September 1811. Cribb, who was the winner, stayed at *The Blue Bull* (*99 miles*), which was a small inn further north at the junction with the South Witham road.

A little further north again, just before the turning to North Witham, there is a large red brick, black-roofed farmhouse on the right-hand side of the road. This was *The Black Bull Inn* (*100¼ miles*) which returned to life as a farm and hunting lodge once the railways ruined the coaching trade. It had long ranges of stables at the rear, now replaced by farm buildings.

Shortly after *The Black Bull* the GNR made a forty five degree turn to the left, abandoning the line of Ermine Street, and passed through Colsterworth (*102½ miles*), the birthplace of Isaac Newton. It has a narrow main street, lined with the last stone-built houses to be seen until much further north.

This was prime fox hunting country and there are numerous

small estates and hunting lodges in the area. The road rises and falls as it passes between Easton House Park and Stoke Rochford Park where there was a '...cascade formed by the water of a single spring that rises here from a bed of lime-stone, and discharges full 19 tons in a minute.' (*Paterson's Roads*). The next village was Great Ponton (*106¾ miles*) with its *Blue Horse* inn.

The road down into Grantham (*110¼ miles*) is a long and steep descent into the valley of the River Witham. 'Now the stone buildings begin to give way to brick,' as Colonel Byng observed.

The town grew rapidly with the arrival of the railway and it presents a very Victorian, red brick, appearance now. The tall church spire is 280 feet high and can be seen for miles around, creating a landmark for travellers. Grantham also retains the oldest inn in England, dating from c1200 – *The Angel* which is in the High Street opposite the second turning to Market Place as you travel north. It was patronised by Colonel Byng in May 1792 – 'A very tolerable inn with good stabling.'

The other major coaching inn, the red brick 18th century *George*, is now a shopping centre and is on the other side of the road to *The Angel*, a little further south, just before the first turning to Market Place. The old *George* burned down in 1780 and was rebuilt to take advantage of the rise of the coaching trade. The Edinburgh mail coach would arrive at 7.23 am and the sleepy passengers had forty minutes for a quick wash and breakfast.

Grantham to Doncaster

Leave Grantham on the B1174 to the A1. Turn off following signs to Foston and go through Long Bennington. Rejoin A1. Take the

B6326 into Newark. Leave on the A616, then B6325 through South & North Muskham, and return to A1. Leave on B1164 through Sutton on Trent and Weston, under A1 through Tuxford. Cross A1 to A638. Go through Markham Moor, Retford, Barnby Moor, Ranskill, Scrooby. Take the A614 into Bawtry. Leave on A638 to Rossington Bridge. At the ring road (A18) go straight ahead into Doncaster.

*

The GNR leaves Grantham by Little Gonerby, now absorbed into the town, and up the long slope of Gonerby Hill to Great Gonerby (*112 miles*) which stands on the crest. Its coaching inn, *The Rutland Arms*, has vanished and only the fine church with its spire is left from its earlier days.

The view north as the GNR leaves the village was described by the 18th century clergyman Thomas Twining in 1776. 'You have a view, somewhat sublime and striking from its mere extent and suddenness; but it is as flat as a pancake. The road is through level, Moorish, unpleasant ground from the bottom of that hill to Newark, but, as a road, excellent.'

Colonel Byng thought that, 'the view from Gonerby Hill is very extensive but not of beauty; all wide views are horrors to me, like an embankment into Eternity.'

Gonerby was where Oliver Cromwell's rise to power began with a victory over the Royalists in May 1643. The hill down to the north is supposed to have been the steepest part of the GNR, although it was improved by a cutting at the crest. It features in fiction in Walter Scott's *Heart of Midlothian* (1818) where Jeanie

Deans walks from Edinburgh to London and encounters thieves and murderers at its foot. Harrison Ainsworth in *Rookwood* (1838) has Dick Turpin cresting the hill only to be faced, prophetically, with a gibbet holding two mouldering corpses.

The two villages of Foston (*116 miles*) and Long Bennington (*118¼ miles*) had little to distract the traveller as they passed over the featureless and flat twelve miles towards Newark, crossing into Nottinghamshire over Shire Dyke (*120½ miles*). 'The road becomes of a gravelly amendment; so both man and horse jog on at their own ease.' (Byng)

The GNR descended to the valley of the Trent through Balderton (*122¼ miles*), a long, and not very exciting, approach to the interesting town of Newark (*124½ miles*). The castle, dating back to the 12th century, was where King John died in 1216. James I stayed there as he travelled south to take over the throne of England and it was a Royalist stronghold throughout the English Civil War. From the southern approach it is invisible today, but it is a striking landmark from the north.

For the modern traveller it is best to park as close to the town centre as possible, although the stagecoach would have swept its passengers directly into the market square. The large square retains its size and good view of the church and still has a weekly market. It is surrounded by many surviving old houses and a fine town hall built in 1773 on the site of two of Newark's numerous inns.

Colonel Byng was tempted out to view it in the moonlight – 'a very showy, *grand' place*. I wish there had been soldiers to set it off... Newark church is a noble building, with a noble spire.'

The two chief coaching and posting inns mentioned in *Paterson's Roads* survive. *The Clinton Arms* is on the south side and is still very imposing and *The Saracen's Head* also remains. The effigy of the head is still there, although the building has been much modernised. Sir Walter Scott refers to it as Newark's principal inn.

Lord Byron often stayed at *The Clinton Arms*, then called *The Kingston Arms,* and mentions it in a letter of 1807. His first publisher, Ridge, had offices at number 39 on the corner of the market and Bridge Street and you can see the handsome door-case and the knocker Byron would have used. Byng also patronised *The Kingston Arms*: the stables were good, his parlour poor, apparently.

Once across the Trent the ground was marshy and criss-crossed by rivulets and ditches and the GNR crossed them on low red-brick bridges: 'an excellent road,' reported Colonel Byng. The main branch of the Trent was crossed at Muskham Bridge and the road continued north through the villages of South and North Muskham (*128 miles*), Cromwell, Carlton on Trent, Sutton on Trent and Weston (*134¾ miles*). 'All this Vale of Newark is rich and populous; the country now rising presents a fine view of Lincoln Cathedral and the Lincolnshire hills.' (Byng)

Just north of Weston was *The Black Lion* (*135½ miles*) on Scarthing Moor, a famous inn, now vanished, as has the moorland, which is now fields. Tuxford (*137¾ miles*) is next, a very small town on an exposed ridge. A 'mean, dirty place' according to Byng. It has a fine church and, opposite it, *The Newcastle Arms*, which must have been magnificent in its coaching heyday. As Harper remarked, the whole town seems purposeless without its coaching traffic.

Paterson's Roads notes, 'Tuxford is, according to Gough, "branded to a proverb for its miry situation"… the place is almost made up of inns for the accommodation of travellers.' Byng patronised *The Red Lion*, 'a clean and civil house.'

The road out goes down a hill and then climbs to another ridge with, originally, three windmills on its crest. Colonel Byng admired the fine view of Lincoln and, 'to the north, the prospect becomes very rich and beautiful.' The surviving Tuxford Mill (1810), is still working and can be visited. Over the ridge the road descends to Markham Moor where a toll gate and *The Markham Moor Inn* once stood (*140½ miles*). The Moor was enclosed in 1810 and the whole area is now buried under a massive road junction. There is a *Markham Hotel* close by, but this appears to be Victorian.

Just north of this tangle of modern roundabouts the GNR forks to the right and 'The Old London Road' goes off to the left. This is an ancient variant of the route and meets the GNR at Barnby Moor. On the verge is a strange grey stone pillar without an inscription. Harper speculated that this may be the Rebel Stone mentioned in old county histories.

The next village, on what Byng called, 'a road of beautiful features', is Gamston (*141½ miles*) on the River Idle. It had a paper mill, as did several of the villages around here. The road crosses the Chesterfield canal.

East Retford (*145 miles*), a busy little industrial town, still retains a large market square and its principal coaching inn, *The White Hart*, which also did a lively trade with post chaises. 'Retford, tasting of a navigation and of manufactories, shows in gaiety!' (Byng)

The road climbs from the town to Barnby Moor, a windswept and desolate area with sanctuary for the traveller at *The Blue Bell Inn*, also known as *The Barnby Moor Inn* (*148 miles*). This is now called *Ye Old Bell*, and gives a good impression of the size it must have been when the stables occupied the car parking space at the rear and accommodated 120 horses.

In 1776 the Revd. Thomas Twining noted that it was a 'gentlemanlike, comfortable house', and in the mid-18th century Lawrence Sterne wrote, 'I am worn out, but press on to Barnby Moor tonight.' Byng found it had, 'A civil landlord, and a good parlour... a good bed in a good bedchamber.'

Colonel Byng had a sore chest, perhaps because of damp weather, and reports having 'snail tea for breakfast' as a cure. It is not clear whether this was some concoction using real snails or whether it was a form of green tea. His bill for the night's lodging and food was eight shillings and eight pence.

As the GNR reaches Scrooby (*152 miles*) the traveller is in Yorkshire. The turnpike keeper and his mother were murdered here by a shepherd called John Spencer who was afterwards hanged and gibbeted at the scene of the crime – the road passes Gibbet Hill Lane just after the village.

Bawtry (*153½ miles*), the next little town, has a long, wide

High Street, ideal for serving the coaches that changed horses here. *The Crown Hotel* still dominates the street and still calls itself a 'posting house' and there are some nice old shop fronts.

Coach travellers were particularly interested in the homes of the nobility and gentry that they passed and all the road books give details. When they could not be seen it was a disappointment: *Paterson's Roads* notes of Bawtry that it is the location of, '…the elegant mansion of the Dowager Lady Galway [which] would have a fine effect were it not surrounded by a high wall, by which it is almost secluded from public view.'

Once out of the town there was a good level road past Rossington Park which could be taken at a brisk pace as far as Rossington Bridge (*157¾ miles*). The inn at the bridge over the River Thorne closed when the railways depressed trade, but is now open again as *The Hare and Tortoise*.

The road rises gently after the bridge and the road is soon running through the modern outskirts of Doncaster. This would have been open countryside in the 18th and early 19th centuries. The road descends to the racecourse (*161 miles*) on Old Town Moor where races have been held since at least 1600. The *St Leger* was established in 1778 and has been a huge draw ever since.

'Doncaster looks well in approach and is a well-built, well-paved, well-streeted town.' (Byng)

The GNR runs straight on towards the town centre (*162¼ miles*), passing through Hall Cross Hill and South Parade where many fine late Georgian and Regency houses remain, including a house where the Prince Regent stayed when visiting the races. The old inns, however, have vanished.

Colonel Byng stayed at *The Angel* and found to be, 'nasty, insolent and with city stabling.' The food was poor too.

Leaving Doncaster on what is now the A638 the road crosses the River Don and splits. The A19 is the branch of the GNR to York. The A638 is the direct route north to Northallerton where the road from York road joins again.

To take the York road first:

Doncaster to York

Leave Doncaster on A638, cross the river and take A19 at roundabout. Continue on A19 into York.

*

The route via York runs through the village of Bentley (*164 miles*), now simply a suburb over what is a flat, and was, a very wet and lonely area, via Owston to Askerne (*169¼ miles*). In the 19th century this was a local spa with a boating lake and a pump room dispensing sulphurous waters. The lake remains by the side of the road but the spa and baths disappeared once the village became a coal mining centre.

The thirteen miles between Askerne and Selby are featureless and wet. Harper, from the viewpoint of the cyclist, which must have been very much like that of a rider or carriage driver, complains that this is '…a flat, watery, treeless, featureless plain, its negative qualities tempered by the frankly mean and ugly villages on the way…' The early maps show large numbers of drains clearing the waters that flow slowly towards the rivers Ouse and Aire.

Whitley was a long, thin straggling village, sticking to the slightly higher ground either side of the road which shortly (*175 miles*) crosses the Knottingley and Goole Canal, opened in 1826 to improve outlets to the coast for the West Yorkshire textile industries.

Egborough on the far side was a mere hamlet and the road continued through it to cross the River Aire at Chapel Haddlesey (*175½ miles*) which does not appear to have grown since coaching days.

Just before Brayton (*180¾ miles*) the road crosses the Selby Canal, completed in 1778 to improve the Aire and Calder Navigation with a short bypass section. Before the canal Selby had been the head of navigation on the Ouse, after it opened traffic could penetrate further into the industrial areas of Yorkshire. This greatly improved the economy of Selby which opened a customs house so ships could go straight out to sea without stopping at Hull. Staithes, warehouses, a counting house, sail and rope makers' shops and cranes were added as the traffic increased. Large Humber keels, brigs, schooners and sloops, some as large as 200 tons, used the canal and must have provided a scene of great interest for the coach travellers.

The church spire of Brayton is an ancient waymark for travellers in what, during the Middle Ages, was a perilous and swampy area. You pass the church on the left and on the northern corner of the next road on the right is a surviving toll house, partly hidden by a hedge.

The road continues into Selby (*182¼ miles*) and sweeps

through it up to the old market area in front of the magnificent abbey church. To the left is the large *Londesborough Hotel*, ideally placed to catch most of the coaching and post chaise business.

Charles G. Harper was not much impressed by early 20th century Selby. Although he found the church and market place attractive he wrote of, 'Mean old houses of no great age; mean new ones; mean and threadbare waterside industries; second-hand clothes shops; coal grit, muddy waters and foreshores of the slimy Ouse, shabby rope walks and dirty alleys: these are Selby.'

Selby was the centre of serious riots against the tollgates in the mid-18th century and in May 1753 a mob gathered one midnight and destroyed all the gates in the area. The militia were needed to quell the uprising and several men were sent to York Castle for trial.

The GNR crosses the Great Ouse then skirts the river through Barlby (*183¾ miles*), Riccall (*186 miles*) and Escrick (*189¼ miles*) and finally reaches the outskirts of York at Fulford, shown as Gate Fulford (*195 miles*) on the old maps. The long built-up suburb of today was then market gardens with some open spaces, a cavalry barracks and scattered cottages until the road arrived at Fishergate. At this point the castle was in sight and the road crossed the River Foss bridge into the city centre (*196¾ miles*).

York was a major destination for travellers and became, as Harper says, almost a third capital city between London and Edinburgh. It would have been an important destination in its own right as well as a focus for 19th century tourists.

London coaches departed from *The Black Swan* in Coney Street. It had a sixty foot frontage onto the street and stabled 130 horses. The first coach service used the inn in 1707 and in 1830 eighteen coaches a day left from *The Black Swan* alone.

Percy Bysshe Shelley, the poet, stayed at there in October 1811, but he had a long coach journey, was very tired and the sight of York Minster was 'lost on him'. Alfred, Lord Tennyson stayed there on 7 July 1852 when it was serving as the headquarters of the Tory party during the general election; 'Great racket, shutters up. Had to get in through a brawling mob to get back for my dinner.' The building has been lost to street widening, although its handsome sign is in the Castle Museum.

The Mail used *The York Tavern* in St Helen's Square where the last Mail coach arrived in 1842 with a black flag flying from its roof, a victim of the legislation allowing the railways to carry the mail.

Colonel Byng stayed at *The George* in Coney Street, in June 1792, 'which inn is one of those very old houses whose front is adorn'd by stucco'd imagery and in it is a very grand apartment with much carved work.' He stayed one night, admired the Minster, was sardonic on the use of the Castle as a prison and sneered at the Assembly Rooms. 'After another good dinner and a good bottle of port wine at the Civil George Inn, I took my leave of York...'

In 1849 Anne and Charlotte Brontë stayed at *The George* on their way to Scarborough because Anne, dying of consumption, wanted to visit the Minster. Despite its magnificence the inn was demolished twenty years later and the only remains are a column and a bay window incorporated into number 17, Colney Street. Some of the building's medieval timber is in the Yorkshire Museum.

York to Northallerton

Leave York on the A19. Enter Easingwold on York Road, turn left on to Long Street (becoming Thirsk Road) to rejoin A2. Take A61 into centre of Thirsk and turn left for Market Square. Leave on A168 to Northallerton. At Northallerton go straight ahead into the High Street (B1333).

*

The GNR leaves York by Bootham Bar where the medieval gate still stands. The road passes through Clifton, originally a separate village which became a prosperous suburb during the 19th century. The road runs level and flat through farmland that was once the wild Forest of Galtres until it reaches Easingwold (*210¼ miles*), now by-passed by the modern road. The aptly named Long Street is the main thoroughfare where the two main coaching inns stood. *The Rose and Crown,* which has vanished, kept five post boys and also horsed the *Wellington* and *Express* coaches for the stage to Thirsk. *The New Inn,* still there at number 62, was where the Mail coaches and the *Highflyer* changed horses.

The road out of town is a long, gentle hill. Just before it rejoins the modern road it passes between two whitewashed buildings, part of White House Farm. This used to be *The White House* inn (*211¾ miles*) and was the scene of an infamous murder in 1623. The innkeeper, Ralph Raynard, was having an affair with an old flame who had married a local farmer called Fletcher. Raynard, his ostler and Mrs Fletcher drowned Fletcher in the Kyle Brook, just up the road, then buried him in the garden of the *White House*. Eventually Raynard's conscience got the better of him, he was convinced he was being haunted by the ghost of the dead man and he confessed.

All three murderers were hanged and gibbeted close to the scene of the crime. Immediately after the old road joins the bypass it crosses a narrow stream, the Kyle Brook where Fletcher was drowned.

The GNR runs on, rising and falling more as the edge of the North York Moors approaches, with views of the Hambledon Hills to the right. Shortly after the right turns to Great and Little Thirkleby it passes the handsome gates of Thirkleby Hall, a substantial 18th century mansion demolished in 1927. *The Griffin* Inn used to stand opposite the gates, but with Thirsk so close this can only have been for the convenience of the farmers and drovers passing the toll gate at this point.

Thirsk (*220½ miles*) has a lively market square where the town's two major coaching inns, *The Three Tuns* and *The Golden Fleece* are still in business. Harper, who seems to have taken against Yorkshire generally, says, 'they show their hard faces to the grey, gaunt streets.' Perhaps the gauntness was the result of the decline after the arrival of the railways.

Three miles north of Thirsk the road bends sharply to the left, just by the tiny church of Thornton le Street (*223½ miles*). The original route went straight on here and it is worth driving into the hamlet and parking to see the 12th century church and *The Spotted* Dog inn, now converted to houses on both sides of the little street. The road continued into what are now fields.

The new route goes down the hill, round the bend, past the gates to the Hall and then past the farm entrance on the right where the old road.

The road climbs back to the crest and continues, with little interruption, to Northallerton (*229¼ miles*). The town has an impressively long and wide High Street, designed to accommodate a large market and deal with a busy passing carriage trade. The two main coaching inns survive. *The Golden Lion* was the more important and the London to Newcastle coach, *The Wellington*, changed horses there while *The Black Bull* horsed the Mail. Northallerton was an administrative and commercial centre rather than an industrial town and derived much of its prosperity from the GNR.

At Northallerton the branch of the GNR that went straight on at Doncaster joins the York branch, so we now return to Doncaster to follow the direct route.

Doncaster to Wetherby

Leave Doncaster on the A638. Join A1 at the Red House interchange. Divert through Wentbridge on the B6474 and rejoin A1. Take A162 into Ferrybridge. Just before the bridge over the River Aire take the slip road to the left signposted Ferrybridge B6136. At the crossroads go straight over onto Old Great North Road and park to see the bridge. Retrace route and rejoin A612, cross the river and take first exit onto Old Great North Road (by Indian restaurant). Join A1246 to A63. At the next roundabout go straight on onto Great North Road into Micklefield. Continue and cross B1217 to Aberford. Keep on minor road next to A1(M) to roundabout with A64. Take 3rd exit and continue on A168 running next to A1(M) to Bramham. Cross A1(M) and continue north on A168 and B6164 into Wetherby.

*

It seems strange to be leaving on York Road, given that the York branch of the GNR is now the A19, but we are now following the beginning of the older route before road improvements at the end of the 18th century made the Selby road to York easier. The junction with the A635 was the York Bar (*164 miles*) where there was a toll gate and a small inn, the predecessor of the modern one in the same location. The road then climbs to the site of Barnsdale Bar where five routes meet and where some of the Leeds coaches took the left-hand road, now A639.

The road winds its way over hilly country to the Red House junction with the A1 (*167¼ miles*). Originally there was a real *Red House* here, a small inn painted bright red and serving the traffic along the Wakefield road. It is now a farm.

A few miles north is Robin Hood's Well (*169¼ miles*), supposedly the spot where Robin Hood accosted the Bishop of Hereford and made him dance a jig. It can be glimpsed at the end of a long lay-by off the southbound carriageway, but there is no easy way of visiting it without a detour if one is travelling north.

In the 17th century John Evelyn described a stone seat and a dipper to drink from the well. The monument, designed by Vanborough, was erected in the early 18th century on the orders of the Earl of Carlisle. Before the A1 was widened there was a small hamlet and two inns here, *The New Inn* and *The Robin Hood*.

At Wentbridge (*172¾ miles*) we turn off the modern road to experience one of the more alarming plunges on the GNR, down into the pretty, steep-sided valley of the River Went where not only did the passengers on the roof have to cling on for dear life going down but they were likely to be turned off to walk up the other side to spare the horses. In the later years of coaching the hill was eased slightly with cuttings.

Harper describes the road from here to Ferrybridge as, 'bleak, high, tableland' and recalls the damage done when the numerous streams and small rivers in the area flooded, carrying away bridges.

It is not easy to picture Ferrybridge (*177½ miles*) as it was when the road dropped down steeply into the valley of the Aire instead of being carried over a high bridge, but the elegant little toll house before the early 18th century stone bridge remains, even though the bridge is closed to traffic.

Ferrybridge, which is where the oldest alternative route to York branches off, had two magnificent coaching inns. *The Swan* was considered to be the most luxurious in the north of England and, as Sir Walter Scott wrote, '…in 1737 and since the best inn upon the great northern road.' Its rival *The Angel* was judged to be the largest inn on the road. The town was so busy that it could support two more significant inns, *The Greyhound* and *The Golden Lion*.

Colonel Byng stayed at *The Angel* in 1792 and was very impressed. He walked around the river banks, admired the bridge, rode out to view the countryside and was helped to plan his next stage by Mr Denton the landlord's supply of maps and prints.

Leaving Ferrybridge we fork left at a roundabout where the road divides, with the old route to York via Tadcaster going off to the right (A162) and the GNR going left (Old Great North Road.) An Indian restaurant occupies the site where *The Old Fox*, a drovers' inn, used to be. On the early maps this is Brotherton, although the little hamlet of Byram seems to have swamped it in modern times. (*178½ miles*)

Harper says of the road out of Brotherton, 'It is a wild, weird kind of country upon which we enter... Away to the left suddenly opens a wide valley, in an almost sheer drop from the road, looking out upon illimitable perspectives.' The area is pockmarked with limestone quarries, as it was in the 19th century.

The A63, leaving to the left, was the Peckford turnpike where the Leeds and London coaches turned off – the Royal Mail, *Rockingham* and *Union Post*. The house just before the modern roundabout may be the old *Boot and Shoe* inn that stood on the junction, although, if it is, it has been heavily modernised.

The road runs into New Micklefield, a hamlet that developed when the railway was put in by the quarry company, and then into Micklefield itself (*184 miles*). The village retains some of its old stone cottages and has lost the smoke, coal dust and hauling gear that came with coal mining in the later 19th century.

The road rises from the valley of the little She Dike to the higher ground of Hook Moor where it joins Ermine Street and passes the lodge gates of Parlington Hall on the left. Parlington was the home of the Gascoigne family from 1546 until 1905 when the new heir, ruined by death duties, simply abandoned it to rot and it was mostly dismantled and sold off.

As the GNR descends the long gentle hill into Aberford it passes some dramatic Gothic alms-houses on the left which, ancient as they seem, were built in the 1840s and would not have been a landmark for the coach passengers.

The village itself (*186½ miles*) centres around the bridge over the little River Cock and the steepness of the hill increases abruptly as it approaches it, passing the handsome white front of *The Swan* where the Carlisle and Glasgow mail coach would change horses. Across the bridge, on the other side of the road, *The Arabian Horse* overlooks the pleasant village green.

The road undulates across rolling country here, rising to windswept Bramham Moor (*189 miles*) where *The White Horse* inn stood at the crossroads with the Tadcaster-Leeds road, now lost under the modern motorway junction.

The A1 bypasses Bramham village (*190¼ miles*), reducing the impact of the steep hill out of the village, and on to Moor End. From here the road descended in a long hill to the valley of the River Wharfe and the town of Wetherby, 194½ miles north of London and virtually halfway on the road to Edinburgh.

Harper describes Wetherby as a 'hard faced, stony town', and notes that it was always a major centre for cattle rearing and dealing and had crowded stock markets.

The old stone bridge is long and fairly level, no great challenge to the coaches which would run straight on and up the moderate hill of the High Street, passing numerous little ale houses on their way to *The Angel*, the main coaching inn. It is now the *Sant' Angelo* restaurant. *The Angel* called itself the 'halfway house', although the true halfway point between London and Edinburgh actually comes a little further north.

'This Angel Inn at Wetherby I should highly recommend for its civility, cheapness and good cookery; they take in both the morning and evening papers; which become a wonderful treat at this distance from London,' wrote Colonel Byng who arrived there on 6 June 1792.

The London and Glasgow mail coaches going north stopped at *The Angel* for an hour for the passengers to snatch dinner while the southbound ones went on to Aberford to dine. Ferrybridge to Wetherby was one stage for the stagecoaches, which must have left the horses slow and exhausted by the time they reached *The Angel*, or, a little further along on the same side, *The Swan and Talbot*, an older inn which also survives.

Wetherby to Northallerton

A168 to Boroughbridge. Take the minor road signposted to Boroughbridge. Leave on B6265 to rejoin A168. Turn off on slip road to Asenby into Topcliffe. Leave on A167. At Northallerton take the B1333 into the High Street.

The real halfway point on the GNR was at *The Fox Inn*, now vanished, a drovers' inn just north of the turning to Kirk Deighton (*195¼ miles*). From here the road sweeps on to cross the River Nidd at Walshford (*197¼ miles*). The old bridge was to the left of the present one and the road ran past the gates of the Ribstone estate to pass *The Walshford Bridge* inn, a large posting house, on the far side from the modern road.

The A1 has partly obliterated the line of the GNR, but we can take the A168 which parallels it. Just after crossing the railway line there is a farm road to the left, under the A1, to what was *The New Inn* where the Mail coaches changed horses. It has long since become a farm, which is what it probably was originally.

Back on the A168, the GNR passes the long brick walls of Allerton Park (*200¾ miles*) before reaching Boroughbridge (*206¼ miles*) close by the Roman town of Isurium, which would have interested any antiquarian travellers. The road crosses the small tributary of the River Tutt before entering the long street, Horsefair, that runs all the way to the bridge over the River Ure. Old Boroughbridge in the coaching days was entirely south of the river. It had twenty two inns and ale houses, but the two main coaching inns were *The Crown*, which is still in use and *The Greyhounds* which stands opposite, now converted into flats and given a Georgian-style makeover which has done away with its old entrance.

Boroughbridge was an important crossroads which made it an exceptionally busy coaching town. *The Crown* alone could stable one hundred horses. Coaches for Glasgow left the GNR here and it was also a hub for the 'short-stage' coaches serving Knaresborough, Ripon and Harrogate.

The bridge over the Ure was built in the late 18th century by Metcalfe the blind road and bridge maker. Ermine Street forks to the left once over the bridge, cutting an almost straight line north towards Richmond and Scotch Corner while the GNR took the right fork. However, Dishforth airfield now sits right across the course of the road, which makes it impossible to retrace it accurately. The best approach is to take the left fork and to parallel the A1 until the road turns towards Asenby and rejoins the GNR route.

Asenby (*212¼ miles*) is separated from Topcliffe by the River Swale. The road descends to a right-angle turn onto the stone bridge, which must have required skilful driving, and then rises to the ridge on the far side.

From there to Northallerton the GNR winds through farmland giving the impression that it has not changed much in width, line or gradient since the coaching days. The old *Bushey Stoop* inn still stands at the junction of the Thirsk road (now A61) and from Kirkby Wiske onwards the route follows the little River Wiske until we reach Northallerton (*225¼ miles*) where the two arms of the GNR join up again.

Northallerton to Darlington

A167 to Darlington

*

The road to Darlington is only about 16 miles but is a

complete contrast to the long straight run into Northallerton. The road rises and falls over low hills and makes several right-angle turns before reaching the River Tees.

The first small landmark is the tiny hamlet of Lovesome Hill (*229¾ miles*) where an inn once stood. The next hostelry was *The Salutation*, also now vanished, before the road crosses the River Wiske and turns sharp left into Great Smeaton (*232¾ miles*) whose main street runs along the top of a low rise. This is where the Mail coaches changed horses, giving a short stage – seven miles to Northallerton or nine to Darlington. The inn was *The Blacksmith's Arms* which in 1903 Harper said, 'has long since been converted into cottages.'

The road turns sharp right out of the village and on to High and then Low Entercommon (*233¾ miles*). Although both the 'High' and the 'Low' are relatively slight, the location was wild and remote with a lonely tollgate at the junction with the turning to Kirk Levington and *The Golden Lion* inn which stabled horses for the coaches that made a long stage from Northallerton.

The road makes a sharp left at Low Entercommon and then right again – both smoothed out now by the modern road-maker – to make for the crossing of the Tees at Croft. The village of Dalton Upon Tees (*236¾ miles*), bypassed by the modern road, was only a little hamlet with a green and an ale house, but the next village, Croft, was, for a short time in the 18th century, a minor resort of fashion with a racecourse and a spa.

Croft (*237¾ miles*) has a magnificent bridge of seven arches built in the late 17th century to link the Yorkshire and Durham banks of the Tees. Facing the bridge is *The Croft Hotel*, the location of the spa, its size testifying to the brief popularity of the resort. There was a racecourse, now simply a field, and a number of prosperous houses tucked away behind high walls and hedges, but the little village with its sulphurous waters could not compete with the elegancies of Harrogate.

The road enters County Durham on the far side of the bridge and, as it turns north, passes one of those features that provided scope for local legends and stories to entertain bored coach passengers. The GNR follows the bend of the river over the tributary River Skerne and in a pasture to the right, just at the next bend, are two deep pools known as Hell's Kettles. Unfortunately they are no longer visible from the road so the modern traveller cannot peer into their depths and see the impious farmer and his plough team who were swallowed up for working on St Barnabas's Day. Daniel Defoe would have none of it. ''Tis evident they are nothing but old coal-pits, filled with water by the River Tees.'

Harper is snobbish about Darlington's (*241¾ miles*) prosperity at the turn of the 20th century when shabby old houses were shoulder to shoulder with glittering new stores, public houses and civic buildings. In the coaching days, before its pioneering railway brought it prosperity, it was generally considered a small and very dirty town.

Coach travellers might be entertained by a glimpse of the Stockton and Darlington railway, begun in May 1822 when the use of a steam engines was not envisaged. Nor were passengers planned for, as this was to be a horse-drawn railway for moving coal. However, Stephenson's *Locomotive* transformed expectations and the first train of wagons travelled at up to twelve miles an hour.

Passengers were transported shortly after the opening in a horse-drawn wagon dubbed *The Experiment* which travelled the twelve miles in two hours. Various other vehicles were tried, including old stagecoach bodies on wheels, and the first steam-drawn passenger train raced a stagecoach over a twelve mile course and won by 120 yards. Not surprisingly there is little to be seen in modern Darlington that would recall coaching days.

Darlington to Durham

Leave Darlington on A167. At Ferryhill take B6287 through the village to rejoin A167. At Sunderland Bridge, cross the river, turn left onto B6300 and next left to the old bridge. Return to A167 and continue to A177 to Durham.

*

The road rises steadily away from Darlington to a crest at Coatham Mundeville (*245¾ miles*) where the summit was crowned, as now, by a small inn and a few 18th century houses.

Aycliffe village (*246¾ miles*) is bypassed by the modern road, but it is easy to drive through the old village which must look, with its green and the attractive cottages, much as nineteenth century travellers would have seen it. Newton Aycliffe to the left of the road is an entirely 19th century development.

Just after the road passes over a disused railway line is the modern *Gretna Inn* on the site of the old *Gretna Green Wedding*

Inn. Opposite was *The Bay Horse*, originally *The Traveller's Rest*. (*248 miles*) *The Gretna Green Wedding Inn* reminds us that there were several routes leading to Gretna for eloping couples although, of course, any road that took them over the Scottish border would do for their purposes.

A little further on is Rushyford (*250½ miles*), described by Harper as, '…Rushyford Bridge, a pretty scene, where a little tributary of the Skerne prattles over its stony bed and disappears under the road beside that old-time posting-house and inn, the Wheatsheaf.'

Sadly a roundabout sits firmly in the middle of this once-idyllic spot and *The Wheatsheaf* is now *The Eden Arms Hotel*, much modernised and changed. Lord Eldon, the Prince Regent's Lord Chancellor, often visited *The Wheatsheaf* where he maintained his own wine cellar and a large stock of Carbonell's *Fine Old Military Port*. The story goes that he and the landlord would consume seven bottles a day between them.

The next village is Ferryhill (*253 miles*), a coal mining community perched on a ridge looking out over the Wear valley to the north. The modern road leaves the village on the right and plunges downhill using a cutting that was begun in the 19th century to improve the road for the coaching traffic but was halted by the arrival of the railways before it was finished. It was only later in the century that it was competed. To experience the alarming descent as the coach passengers must have done, take the road into the village, turn sharply downhill and rejoin the modern road at the foot.

The passengers would have been distracted from their fears over the steep descent by a truly gruesome tale at the next village, Thinford. In 1685 three children were murdered by a simple-minded youth called Andrew Mills who was not only hanged for the crime but then placed, while still alive, in the gibbet which stood near *Thinford Inn*. Even worse, it was fitted with an iron spike under his chin so he could not eat and his sweetheart misguidedly kept him alive for days by giving him milk while the neighbourhood was rendered hideous by his groans. The gibbet-post was afterwards known as *Andrew Mills' Stob* and splinters of the wood were reputed to be effective against toothache, rheumatism and just about any other malady the locals could think of until, years later, it was finally chipped away to nothing.

The next-but-one roundabout, in Croxdale (*255 miles*), has obliterated another gallows site where highwayman Andrew Tate was hanged in 1602 for the robbery and murder of seven people near Sunderland Bridge.

The road descends into the valley of the River Wear. Immediately after the right turn to the village of Sunderland Bridge (*255¾ miles*), look to the left to see the blocked-off old road descending precipitously to the river. The old bridge can be reached by taking the first left after the crossing, then turning left again.

The bridge is a handsome stone structure, but the steepness of the bank on the southern approach is alarming. In 1822 the mail coach overturned here and two passengers died. Once across the bridge the road turned sharp right along what is now the front drive of a private house.

The GNR continues to Farewell Hill where the long road down to Durham begins and the outside passengers, like ancient pilgrims, would have caught their first glimpse of the cathedral.

Durham to Newcastle

Enter Durham on the A177 and park at the Park & Ride which takes you into the city to Elvet bridge. Leave down New Elvet, cross the river, turn left at roundabout onto A690 following signs for Consett. Cross the river again, turn right at the roundabout up the hill towards A691 and the Consett direction. At the roundabout take B6532 to Framwellgate Moor. At the 2nd roundabout take the minor road to Framwellgate Moor and Pity Me to A167. At Chester le Street go through the town centre on Durham Road, across A693 and continue on A167 through Gateshead. Follow signs to Swing Bridge to cross the Tyne into Newcastle.

*

The easiest way to explore Durham (*260 miles*) is to take the Park & Ride that you pass on your way down the hill and then get off at Elvet Bridge. The bus drops you fittingly at *The Three Tuns*, the main coaching inn.

Durham would have been a major destination for tourists, businessmen and clerics as it is today, with the castle and the cathedral, both on Palace Green, as the principal sights. To leave the city the GNR crosses the River Wear twice, then climbs to Framwellgate Moor (*261 miles*) and runs through Pity Me (named for a local inn with the sign of a hunted fox) on to Chester le Street. Nothing can be seen of the original tiny hamlet, now covered in the red brick terraces built to house coal miners and their families.

The road on from Pity Me runs through what is farmland now, but was originally moor, on a low ridge between the River Wear and the Black Burn. At Chester le Street (*266 miles*) the GNR goes straight on at the first roundabout. To visit Lumley Castle, now a hotel, continue on the A167, then right at the next roundabout onto B1284, over the river and first left past the golf club.

Returning to the GNR through Chester le Street there is no trace of what Defoe called, 'an old dirty thoroughfare town', or of coaching days. The old town was linear, reaching as far as the Chester Burn, now channelled beneath modern roads and car parks, just south of the junction with B6313. Once past that point the traveller passed through three and a half miles of open ground with wide views of the Durham countryside, pockmarked with the chimneys and hoisting gear of the scattered collieries. Now the road is built up all the way to the Angel of the North junction, but in the late 18th century Birtley (*269 miles*) was the only village along that stretch, situated to the right of the GNR with a colliery and an iron works close at hand.

The modern junction with the A1 is massive and gives the impression that this must be an historic crossroads of some importance. In fact there were only minor roads going off to east and west at this point and the A1's route bypasses Newcastle over more or less virgin terrain.

From the junction the GNR begins to climb to the ridge

overlooking the Tyne. For a short distance it is over open ground, then the suburbs begin that run all the way to Gateshead. A mile from the A1 junction the GNR passes over another road. This is Harlow Green Lane and Harper's description of it in about 1900 shows how much change there has been. 'At Harlowgreen Lane, where a little wayside inn, the 'Coach and Horses', stands beside a wooded dingle, we have the only pleasant spot before reaching Gateshead. Prettily rural, with an old-world air...'

The road rises more to become Gateshead Fell (*271 miles*) which was originally scattered with tiny hamlets and farms. The road itself had several gibbets along the way. The last recorded one was erected in 1770 for the body of highwayman Robert Hazlett who robbed first a young lady travelling by post chaise and then the post boy with his mail sacks. Gateshead itself did not begin until the point where Old Durham Road, an alternative route over the Fell, joined from the right at the point where the B1426 now crosses.

To get the nearest approach to the coach traveller's experience we turn off after the road goes under the railway to take the curiously named Bottle Bank down its scarily steep drop to the river. The landmarks of the castle, cathedral and Moothall on the Newcastle side were the same as the Georgian traveller would have seen before they were pitched down the steep cobbled street. (*273½ miles*)

Newcastle to Morpeth

Leave Newcastle on the B1318 across Town Moor. Continue to A1056 then B1318. At junction with A19 take 2nd exit, unnumbered road. Join A1 after Stannington to next junction A197 to Morpeth.

*

The present Swing Bridge was constructed in 1876 and occupies the same location as the succession of crossings since the Romans. Hadrian built the first bridge in AD122 and the medieval structures that followed used its foundations. The first dateable stone bridge after the Romans was erected in 1248 to replace what seems to have been a wooden one, destroyed by fire. It had ten arches, defensive towers and a drawbridge with portcullis and shops, houses and even a prison. It lasted until 1771 when it was swept away in a flood.

Ferries had to be used until the following year when a temporary bridge was put up, partly on the remains of the old structure, but this was narrow and could carry only a limited weight. The opening of a new bridge in 1781 must have been a huge relief for travellers. It was widened in 1803 and tolls were charged until 1821. But, as the industrial development of the area intensified, the bridge was found to be too low for modern shipping and in 1876 it was replaced by the Swing Bridge, allowing river traffic to move unimpeded. Before then, in 1849, Robert Stephenson had built the High Level bridge that carries both road and rail traffic across without having to descend into the valley at all.

It is no longer possible to follow the GNR through Newcastle (*274½ miles*) by car from the south because of the one-way streets, so to explore on foot you can park on the quayside. The GNR turned right after the bridge to Sandhill and then left to climb the steep hill called Side. On the corner is a fine half-timbered house with a plaque: 'From the above window on Nov 18th 1772 Bessy Surtees descended and eloped with John Scott later created 1st Earl of Eldon and Lord Chancellor of England.'

This is the same Lord Eldon who we met staying at *The Wheatsheaf* at Rushyford Bridge. Ironically Lord Eldon came in for much satirical comment when his own daughter eloped with the architect George S. Repton from Eldon's London house in Bedford Square. His own romance, beginning with this imprudent elopement when he was only twenty one, resulted a marriage across the border at Blackshields and years of frugal living while he clawed his way up as a lawyer.

Side is very steep and curves upwards to St Nicholas Street, with the cathedral just above it. From there it takes a curving line up Groat Market, Bigg Market and Newgate Street before leaving Newcastle across the Town Moor.

The last mail coach left Newcastle in July 1847. In 1901 Harper lamented that none of Newcastle's coaching inns remained, but part of the 18th century *Queen's Head* can be seen by walking along Mosley Street from the cathedral then turning left into Pilgrim Street. The building is on the left with a green porch at the front door. It was Alderman Fenwick's house in 1773 but then became one of the principal coaching inns of the city. It remained a hotel with stables stretching back to Grey Street until 1884 when it became the Liberal Club. It fell into disrepair by the 1960s but has been rescued and restored.

Harper also seems to have missed *The Old George*, a 17th

century inn that had stables and was popular with farmers at the nearby Corn Market. The main sights for travellers would have included the castle, the cathedral, the Moot Hall and the fine Assembly Rooms of 1776.

The GNR left Newcastle across Town Moor with the racecourse to the left and the local beauty spot of Jesmond Dene on the right. Now the racecourse has gone and it looks very tidy and park-like until it reaches the built-up area of Gosforth. In coaching days this was a hamlet called Bulman's Village with a turnpike gate at its northern end.

The road goes on past Gosforth Park (*277 miles*) to North Gosforth, an entirely modern community, and through the colliery villages of Wide Open and Seaton Burn which were mere hamlets at the turn of the 18th and 19th centuries.

Just after crossing the A1, on the left, are the gates to Blagdon Park, seat of the Ridley family for generations. The gates are rather fine and are surmounted by the family crest of white bulls, but these days the carriage drive leads to a vast open-cast mine, scarring the park south of the house. Further north, just past the later 19th century lodge, there is a small rectangular Classical pavilion standing on the other side of the wall of the park. This is the Kale Cross, or market house, which used to stand in the Side in Newcastle until the mid-18th century.

We now have to join the A1 to cross the Black Dene, the River Blythe, one of the numerous little ravines that the GNR had to negotiate from here northwards. A length of the old bridge parapet is visible on the eastern side.

The road down to Morpeth (*289¼ miles*) follows the original GNR in a long descent to the river, which, although gradual until the final steep section, must have been very long pull for coaches travelling south. Just before the bridge is the apparently medieval tower of Morpeth Court which was built in 1821 as a prison and then became a police station.

Today road traffic crosses the Wansbeck by Telford's bridge of 1831, but until then the only option was the narrow, hump-backed medieval bridge to the left where the footbridge now crosses. It was painted by Turner and you can just glimpse an inn sign on the far side which may be for *The Black Bull*. To see the route, take the left fork to Castle Square, park and walk down Wansbeck Street. On the far bank there is an ancient chantry where travellers could pray.

The GNR turned left over the bridge into Bridge Street to pass *The Black Bull* with its prominent rounded full-height bay painted white. There is a very narrow Adam-detailed entrance that led through to the stable yard. As with most of these small entrances, the coach would have stood in the street and the horses, already harnessed, would have been led out to it.

The other old inns are gone, but are remembered in the names of the alleyways as you walk along Bridge Street and Newgate Street: the town obviously once had many hostelries.

Morpeth to the Border

Leave on the A192 to A1. Turn off to go through West Thirston and Felton. Rejoin A1. Take turning to Swarland to Nelson monument, then continue on same road through Newton on the Moor to return to A1. Take A1068 to Alnwick town centre and leave on B6341 to A1. Detour through Warenford to Belford and return to A1 to Berwick. Leave Berwick on North Road to the A1.

*

It is a long, steep pull north out of Morpeth across wild country crossed by burns and dotted with isolated farms and pele towers. Once out of the valley the road runs north through open country with no villages or towns to offer a change of horses and accommodation, only the isolated *Portland Arms Inn*, about halfway on the eleven miles between Morpeth and West Thirston.

West Thirston (*299¼ miles*) lies on the south bank of the River Coquet with Felton immediately over the bridge on the far bank. It is a very steep one in ten drop into valley where the road levels out at *The Northumberland Arms*. The coaches then had to negotiate a right angle turn onto and off the charming stone bridge and up the steep hill through Felton. (*299¾ miles*) Given the length of the stage from Morpeth they would have changed horses here, so at least the team would be fresh to tackle the hill.

The old route signposted to Swarland takes us past what would have been an interesting landmark for travellers after 1807. Just on the left after coming off the A1 is an obelisk erected by Alexander Davison, a merchant, ship owner and banker who was a friend of Nelson. He bought Swarland Park, largely with money gained by selling-off enemy prize ships, and laid out clumps of trees to show the disposition of the French and British fleets at the battle of the Nile. In 1807 he erected the memorial 'to the memory of private friendship.'

The little hamlet of Newton on the Moor (*302½ miles*) is the last settlement before Alnwick (*308½ miles*), a picturesque grey stone town when you reach the middle of it. The ancient castle was drastically 'modernised' in the later 18th century by the first Duke of Northumberland who changed his name to Percy from Smithson on acquiring it by marriage. He asked George III for the Order of the Garter, pointing out that he would be the first Percy to have been refused it. The King, who apparently did not take to the ex-apothecary, retorted, 'You forget, you are the first Smithson who ever asked for it.' The third duke made even more sweeping alterations in 1855 and the castle is now medieval outside and Italianate inside.

Respectable travellers could usually gain admittance to be shown around by the housekeeper when the family was not at home, as was the case with most great country houses. On their way to the castle they would have passed, as we do, the monument to the second duke, erected in 1816 to commemorate the fact that he reduced his tenants' rents in the agricultural depression that followed the peace with France. Harper points out acidly that, as he had doubled them in the war years, this was not much of a concession.

The road out of Alnwick dives steeply down to the River Aln and a stone bridge with a Percy lion at the centre and a good view back up to the castle – another Northumberland bridge painted by Turner.

The road out of the valley is a three-mile climb to Heiferlaw Bank (*310 miles*). The modern road has a roundabout at the end of the first stretch up from the bridge. In the woodland to the right just before it is reached it is possible to see Malcolm's Cross, erected by the Duchess of Northumberland in 1774. It marks the spot where Malcolm III, King of Scotland, was killed in battle in 1093.

From the top of Heiferlaw Bank there is a wide view of the moors with the Cheviot Hills to the north-west. A Mrs Montagu wrote in 1789, 'These moors are not totally uninhabited, but they look unblest.' Travellers must have prayed for good weather before crossing them.

The road descends to more level country through Warenford (*318¾ miles*) to Belford (*323 miles*), a handsome little village with the large *Blue Bell* inn facing the market square. If this was the first change of horses after Alnwick it would have been a long stage, almost sixteen miles.

The GNR is close to the coast now and converging with it as it approaches Berwick on Tweed. The small town on the southern bank of the estuary is Tweedmouth (*337½ miles*) and, although it does not retain anything of particular interest historically, it is worth parking for a view of the spectacular bridge of fifteen arches, built just after James VI of Scotland became James I of England in 1603.

Berwick (*338 miles*) changed hands between the Scots and the English throughout the Middle Ages and was finally established as an English town in 1551. It became a 'county corporate', one of eighteen such entities which were separate from their surrounding county and its government. It lost that status and was incorporated into Northumberland in 1885.

Berwick's unusual status and position on the Scottish border caused the misapprehension with some eloping couples that they could safely get married under Scottish law the moment they had crossed the Tweed. In fact they needed to be past the Lamberton Bar before they were safe.

Once over the bridge, and through the Sally Port in the fortifications, the coaches would have turned right and then left into the wide Hide Hill before turning left, squeezing past the town hall into Marygate, effectively the High Street. Berwick was a busy transport hub and most of the major inns were in this street, although it is not easy to identify any survivors now.

Until 1834 mail coaches in England only permitted three outside passengers, all sitting facing forward so they could not take the guard by surprise and rob his strong box. The mails north from Berwick were allowed four, apparently as a concession to provide more transport in the poorly-provided northern areas.

The Border to Edinburgh

A1 to Lamberton, through the village and rejoin A1 to Ayton. Through the village and rejoin A1. Just before Cockburnspath turn right onto A1107. Take first left to Pease Bay and continue through to rejoin A1 beyond Cockburnspath. Continue on A1 to A1087 into Dunbar. Leave on A1097, then A199. Divert through East Linton. A6093 into Haddington. Leave on A6471 to rejoin A199 to Musselburgh. Leave Musselburgh on B6415 through Joppa and Portobello. Take A1140 towards Edinburgh, joining A1. Left into Meadowbank to Duke's Drive, then Queen's Drive.

Right into Horse Wynd past the front of Holyrood House and left up Canongate.

*

Leaving Berwick, the toll bar at Lamberton (*341 miles*) is reached in two and a half miles and the old toll house can just be identified, much altered into a bungalow, on the left hand side of the road at the entrance to the village. Until the change in the law insisting on a residency qualification came into force in 1856 there was, according to Harper, a sign in the window: 'Ginger beer sold here and marriages performed on the most reasonable terms.'

Although Gretna Green is the most famous of the Scottish marriage destinations for eloping English couples, anywhere was legal once they were over the border and could declare that they were married in front of a witness.

Once clear of Lamberton the road runs very close to the cliff edge and the journey must have been alarming on dark nights or in stormy weather. At Burnmouth (*344 miles*) it swings inland, which must have been a relief. Ayton (*346 miles*), with its long High Street, offered *The Red Lion Inn,* now converted into houses but preserving its massive arches opening into the yard. It can be seen on the left, just after the imposing clock tower.

After Ayton the road runs through the valley of the Eye Water, climbing gently but steadily past Reston, Houndwood (*351¾ miles*) and Grantshouse (*354½ miles*) before negotiating a narrow pass and descending to Cockburnspath (*358 miles*). Two streams cut deep gullies to Pease Burn before the modern road reaches Cockburnspath. The A1 goes straight on and crosses the

Heriot Water at 350 feet. If you take the right turning just before that bridge you come almost immediately to the stub of a track going into the woods. There is a ruined tower in there and the remains of a bridge, but it is hidden in a private wood and whether this is the old bridge at this level is impossible to say for certain.

Continuing down the road takes us to a bridge of 1786 which crosses the Pease Burn at only 126 feet. The road then forks off to cross Heriot Water almost at sea level before running back up to the main road. It seems as though the bridge by the tower is the oldest, replaced in the 18th century by the more circuitous, but probably safer lower route until the modern bridge restored the direct way.

Very shortly afterwards the road has to negotiate Dunglas Burn (*359¼ miles*), another narrow rift. We are closer to the sea here, so the drop is slightly less – about 125 feet, but it is still alarming. There are three road bridges here and the railway. The road sweeps over on a modern bridge, but you can see between it and the rail bridge that there is what looks like a late 19th century stone bridge. On the other side of the railway is an older stone bridge.

The road is tight to the coast all the way to Dunbar now and travellers would have had good views of Bass Rock if the weather was clear. It is, and was, possible to bypass Dunbar, but it is twenty seven miles from Berwick and the first town of any size. The original line of the old road, into or past Dunbar, was though Skateraw, but that is now blocked by factories and quarrying, so we must turn off after that and pick the old road up at Broxburn

(*363½ miles*). This is the battlefield of Dunbar where the Parliamentarians under Cromwell defeated Charles I's Scottish army in 1650.

English travellers would have felt they were most definitely in Scotland when they drove down Dunbar's broad High Street (*365¾ miles*) with its dark red stone houses and whitewashed Tolbooth.

It was a good, level road out of Dunbar to East Linton (*370½ miles*) where the road crosses the River Tyne on a red sandstone bridge that is flat and easy to negotiate. This was the birthplace in 1761 of John Rennie, the pioneering engineer and builder of London Bridge.

Travellers interested in Mary Queen of Scots would have looked out for the ruins of Hailes Castle to the south on the banks of the Tyne where in May 1567 the Earl of Bothwell took Mary, probably against her will, thus precipitating the marriage that took place a week later.

The next little town is Haddington (*376 miles*), a medieval Royal Burgh in the 12th century which still retains a wide and handsome main street. As you approach the town centre down Hardgate, next to the river, you pass the site of the Earl of Bothwell's town house, demolished in 1955 and now a small public open space. The English burned Haddington in 1548 as part of Henry VIII's 'rough wooing' of the little Princess Mary on behalf of his son Edward, almost destroying the church of St Mary's which was not fully restored until the 1970s.

The GNR runs on through the colliery villages of Macmerry

(*381½ miles*) and Tranent (*383¼ miles*), Close to Tranent, to the north, is the battlefield of Prestonpans, the site of Bonnie Prince Charlie's major victory over the Hanoverian forces in September 1745. The 'pans' were salt pans along the coast.

There are fine views over the Firth of Forth as the road descends out of Tranent. Edinburgh itself is not visible, but Arthur's Seat and Calton Hill can be seen on a clear day. The road descends into Musselburgh (*387¼ miles*), a small fishing town on the River Esk, through Joppa (*389¼ miles*), once a separate fishing and salt-producing village, into Portobello (*390 miles*). This was once an area known as Figgate Muir and became a haunt of smugglers. A retired veteran of the capture of Portobello in central America in 1742 built a cottage he called Portobello Hut and the small community developed around it after a valuable clay bed was discovered. By the time stage coach passengers were passing through it was a thriving pottery-producing village.

The sands were excellent for exercising cavalry horses and it was here that the quartermaster of the Edinburgh Light Horse, Walter Scott, was kicked in the head during a drill. Enforced bed-rest allowed him to finish the *Lay of the Last Minstrel*. As late as 1806 it was described in *The Scots Magazine* as, 'a perfect waste covered almost entirely with whins and furze.'

From Portobello onwards the old landscape that the coach travellers would have seen is entirely lost beneath modern developments and there is a choice of possible routes into both the New Town and the old. To take the most romantic approach into the old town the road sweeps round the foot of Salisbury Crags, passes Holyrood House and then takes the steep climb up the Royal Mile to the castle. (*393 miles*)

The Traveller Arrives In Edinburgh

The 18th century traveller arriving in expectation of something like a London inn would have been bitterly disappointed until the development of the New Town gave him modern lodgings. Until then travellers were set down at a stabler's establishment which was focused on dealing with the horses. Passengers had to do the best they could with the so-called inns in Plesance and St Mary's Wynd.

One traveller in 1774 wrote, 'One can scarcely form in imagination the distress of a miserable stranger on his first entrance into this city…on entering the house we were conducted by a poor girl without shoes or stockings…into a room where about twenty Scotch drovers had been regaling themselves with whisky and potatoes. You may guess our amazement when we were informed that this was the best inn in the metropolis, and that we could have no beds unless we had an inclination to sleep together, and in the same room with the company which a stage-coach had that moment discharged.'

Dr Johnson put up at *The White Horse* in Boyd's Close and Boswell visited him there to find him in a towering rage because the waiter had sweetened his lemonade without using tongs for the sugar.

To leave our traveller in more salubrious surroundings, we must imagine him in Edinburgh's earliest hotel. John Neale built the first house in New Town in 1774, situated at the eastern end of Princes Street. He leased the upper floors to James Dun who set up his hotel there. He was so proud of it that he hung a large gilded sign outside – *Dun's Hotel* – until the Lord Provost made him remove it on the grounds that 'hotel' was a foreign word.

The Dover Road

The Dover Road to London has been one of the country's major highways since the Romans established the great naval base of Dubris. Even today, we can still see where, in about AD 200, the weary travellers found accommodation at a *mansio* or official lodging house (http://www.theromanpaintedhouse.org.uk/) before setting out on Watling Street for Londinium.

With Calais only 8 leagues away (27.7 miles), the Dover road was crowded with those wishing to take ship for France, to do business with France or, in times of war, to garrison the coast and man the fleet against the French. In addition to those with business in Dover, Canterbury was the premier pilgrimage destination in England from 1170 when Thomas à Becket was murdered in the cathedral. As a result, throughout the ages, merchants, military men, sailors, pilgrims to Canterbury and travellers would have followed the line of the Roman road as we still do, more or less, today.

In the days of the Mail and stage coaches, travellers could choose from a number of London inns as a starting point for their journey but, whichever they favoured, they could expect to be between nine and ten hours on the road. Exceptionally, in 1836, *The Telegraph* coach was promising eight and a half hours from Oxford Street. In the same year travellers could choose from *The Express* leaving from *The Golden Cross* inn at Charing Cross (where Trafalgar Square is now), *The Union* coach from *The White*

Bear in Piccadilly or *The Phoenix* from *The Green Man and Still*, Oxford Street. The Mail could be joined at either *The Golden Cross* or at the General Post Office in the City.

The Union had departures at 8.30 am, 10.30 am or 6.30 pm, with the night journey taking an hour longer. The others departed at between 7.30 am and 9 am.

Whichever coach you chose, the route would be the same and, until 1819, all the coaches starting from the City would have to cross the chaotic permanent traffic jam that was Old London Bridge.

In 1722 three men were employed to attempt to enforce a 'keep left' rule, the first recorded instance of that form of traffic management in the country. The houses and shops that had stood on Old London Bridge, along with the gates at either end that had displayed the heads of traitors, were removed in 1750, but the basic structure remained, with coaches descending the steep Fish Hill with the Monument to the Great Fire on the left, passing under the clock of the church of St Magnus the Martyr and across to reach Bridge Foot, part of the Borough of Southwark, the start of our journey.

The opening of Southwark Bridge in 1819 gave an alternative, with the routes joining up at the church of St George the Martyr, and the opening of the new London Bridge in August 1831 made the older crossing easier.

Southwark to Deptford

From the southern end of London Bridge continue on the A3 along Borough High Street to the church of St George the Martyr on the left. Turn left onto the A2 (Great Dover Street) and continue to the Bricklayer's Arms one-way system, leaving on the A2 (Old Kent Road).

*

Southwark Cathedral is on the right as we reach Bridgefoot (*0 miles*). Until 1905 it was the church of St Saviour and St Mary Overie and still shelters the handsome tomb of Court poet John Gower, friend of Geoffrey Chaucer whose pilgrims gathered here at Southwark to begin their Canterbury journey.

Southwark was separate from London, a borough in the county of Surrey with Roman and Anglo-Saxon origins. Its government was complex, but much was under the control of the Bishop of Winchester. By the Middle Ages it was notorious as the playground for Londoners. Southwark is where you went for bull and bear baiting, playhouses, brothels – the prostitutes were known as the Bishop of Winchester's geese – and all forms of disreputable pleasures.

Borough High Street running south was lined with inns and you can read their names carved on the pavements as you walk: *The Tabard, The Catherine Wheel, The Boar's Head, The Three Widows* and *The Half Moon* are just a few. Only one of these great galleried inns, *The George*, survives in part and it is still a pub.

Although nowadays the area is full of interest – from the Shard to the foodie heaven of Borough Market – few relics remain that the stagecoach traveller would recognise besides the Cathedral, *The George* inn and Guy's Hospital, founded in 1721. Today you can visit the fascinating, if gruesome, Old Operating

Theatre and Herb Garret opposite (www.thegarret.org.uk) and look into the courtyard of Guy's where the poet John Keats attended lectures to become an apothecary, although he never practiced the profession. A Blue Plaque on no. 8 St Thomas's Street marks Keats' lodgings in 1815-16.

The Marshalsea Prison where Charles Dickens's father was imprisoned for debt in 1824 has gone and so has the Clink Prison which gave its name to the slang term for being in gaol – 'in the Clink' – along with the huge Anchor brewery that helped to quench London's vast thirst.

The stage and Mail coach travellers who had boarded north of the river would sit tight when the coaches stopped at Southwark where, by the early 19th century, it was mainly the heavy goods wagons and pack trains, barred from City streets, that set out from these inns.

The route continued down the High Street to the handsome red brick and stone church of St George the Martyr *(¾ mile)* built 1734-6 on the site of two earlier churches. At the second of these, Henry V, returning from victory at Agincourt, was welcomed by the Aldermen of London. There is a wall of the old Marshalsea prison remaining in the churchyard.

Originally the Dover route involved turning sharp left on the southern edge of the church into the vanished Church Street and then forking immediately right down the Kent Street (now Tabard Street). Until 1750, when Great Dover Street (now the A2) was driven through to by-pass it, Kent Street was a notorious slum. It was so bad that foreign dignitaries visiting London would be driven along it at night to hide its worst horrors. 'To give a bit of Kent Street' meant to use foul language of an extreme sort, worse even than Billingsgate.

The first milestone stood where the southern edge of Kent Street met the new Great Dover Street. Now, with the motorists' eyes on the approaching Bricklayer's Arms one-way system, traffic sweeps past with nothing to mark it.

It was at this point that the road from the Blackfriars' Bridge joined. The new bridge was opened in 1819 and brought an influx of traffic to Southwark and a building boom that saw the population double between 1801 and 1851. Travellers making that crossing would have gone down Great Surrey Street (now A202, Blackfriars' Road) to The Royal Circus where the original obelisk milestone still stands in the middle of the road. Here was the first toll gate on this part of the route which followed the modern A201 (London Road) through what is now the Elephant and Castle one-way system – then simply a crossroads with *The Elephant and Castle* inn on one corner – and along through Walworth to join the Southwark route by *The Bricklayer's Arms*. There was a toll gate before the junction, but the notes on Cary's Survey of the High Roads state: *Gates – pass with Circus ticket etc.*

Now *The Bricklayer's Arms* has vanished under the junction with the A201 and the site of the next landmark for the coach passengers is hidden from the southbound modern driver by the overpass where the A2 and A201 join. To the right, between Mason Street and Townsend Street, was the Asylum for the Deaf and Dumb, a pioneering institution founded in 1792 by the

Reverend John Townsend. The handsome red brick building housed two hundred children who would, until then, have been dismissed as 'idiots' and denied any education or useful employment. The children were taught arithmetic, writing, mechanics, design and various trades. Sign-language was rejected in favour of lip reading. In 1902 the pupils moved to The Royal School for Deaf Children in Margate and the site is now occupied by the Townsend Primary School.

The houses were now just a line along the road with market gardens and meadows behind them. The first tollgate (the 'Green Man gate') was situated where the B203 joins the A2 on the left. Just after that there is a cross roads with the B204 and B214. This was the site of the ford of St Thomas à Watering where a stream cut across the highway and where medieval travellers made their first stop out of London. It was also a place of execution well into the 16th century. Heads and 'quarters' of executed felons and heretics were displayed by the ford as an awful warning. The ghost of the stream can be found in an ornamental lake in a public park to the south of the road.

The road swings eastward (*3¼ miles*) as it enters New Cross, not a village in coaching days but simply a hamlet around the junction of the Dover and Maidstone roads. *The Marquis of Granby* pub (junction of A2 and A20, Lewisham Way) marks the location of the New Cross turnpike gate which, Cary informs us, can be passed with the Green Man ticket.

The travellers were now in Kent and in the countryside heading for Deptford, a compact town wedged between the Dover

Road and the Thames at the bottom of its deep southern bend around the Isle of Dogs.

Deptford, Blackheath and Shooters Hill to Crayford

Continue on the A2. At the major roundabout after the Heath continue straight on onto A207, Shooters Hill Road, and remain on A207 into Crayford.

*

The road from Deptford to Canterbury had been fully turnpiked by 1753, albeit in a piecemeal fashion from 1709 onwards.

Deptford is named for the 'deep ford' where the Ravensbourne enters the Thames and has a fascinating history, although virtually nothing now remains to be seen. Sir Francis Drake was knighted there in 1581 by Queen Elizabeth I after his voyage around the world and in 1593 Christopher Marlowe, poet and spy, was murdered at the house of widow Eleanor Bull amidst mystery that has never been resolved. He is buried in St Nicholas churchyard.

In 1697/8 Peter the Great and his entourage stayed in Sayes Court, Deptford, when visiting the royal dockyards. Sayes Court belonged to diarist John Evelyn who had sub-let it to Captain (later Admiral) John Benbow. One of the servants at the house described the royal entourage as 'right nasty' and they trashed the place. Three hundred windows panes were broken, the furniture smashed up and used as firewood and 'twenty fine pictures very much tore and all frames broke.' Evelyn's much-loved garden was destroyed.

In 1665 Samuel Pepys had commented, 'a lovely noble ground he hath indeed.' Evelyn was awarded £150 compensation by the government.

The Deptford toll gate was located where the road crossed the Ravensbourne river, just at the point where the railway line now crosses the A2 after the junction with the A2209/A2210. The Green Man ticket let travellers pass here too.

The stage and Mail route skirts Deptford and by-passes historic Royal Greenwich completely, becomes Blackheath Road and begins to climb steeply to reach Blackheath itself. Once it was indeed 'black' or bleak, an exposed open tableland surrounded by dense woodland making it a favourite haunt of highwaymen and footpads and a good location for duels. But it was also high and airy, a healthy location for those who preferred to live away from London's smogs and crowds. Enough remain of Georgian and Victorian houses along the way to show that this was once a very desirable area for Londoners to live, once the footpads who infested the heath had been subdued.

When you have reached the top of the hill (*5 miles*) you are on the Heath itself. Until the end of the 15th century it was a popular place for invaders and rebels to camp – the Danes in the 11th century, Wat Tyler and the Peasants' Revolt rebels (1381), Jack Cade's rebels (1450) and in 1497 it was the scene of the battle where Henry VII defeated a band of Cornish rebels.

After that it became a popular spot for the reception of visiting royalty, presumably because of the fine views towards London and the presence of the palace at Greenwich. Henry VIII met Anne of Cleves there when, 'From the tentes to the Parke gate of Greenwyche were all bushes and tyrees cut down, and a large and ample waye made for the shew of all persones.' Charles II was greeted here by Londoners on his return from exile in 1660.

It was also useful for military purposes. In March 1687 John Evelyn wrote, 'I saw a trial of those devilish, murdering, mischief-doing engines called bombs, shot out of a mortar-piece on Blackheath.'

Evelyn, who could be sour about many things, was critical of the annual Blackheath cattle fair '...pretended for the sale of cattle, but I think, in truth, to enrich the new tavern at the bowling-green.'

The heath was also the site of gravel extraction for ships' ballast and as a sporting venue. James I imported golf from Scotland and the first golf club in the country was established on Blackheath so, what with that and the bowling and the military exercises, it is amazing that the highwaymen found a quiet spot to carry on their business.

Reaching the top of the plateau you can see ahead and to the left the handsome red brick Ranger's House. Montagu House, once the home of the Earl of Chesterfield, was virtually next door and it was here that Princess Caroline, the estranged wife of the Prince Regent, lived from 1799 to 1812. Her daughter, Princess Charlotte, lived with a governess at the Ranger's House, in those days the mansion of the Duchess of Brunswick.

Coach travellers would have craned to see the house – Caroline was popular in direct contrast to her husband – but she was also wildly eccentric and was once spotted sitting in the garden, her gorgeous gown hitched up to her knees, and drinking from a pint pot of porter.

The route leaves the Heath at the six mile stone. The road, lined with fine 19th century villas, comes to a vast roundabout where there was the tiny hamlet of Charlton. On the far side of the roundabout, is *The Sun in the Sands* pub, an old landmark. The road begins to climb again and *The Fox Under the Hill* pub on the right was just beyond the seven mile point. The imposing buildings of the old military hospital were built initially to care for the wounded of the Crimean war.

None of this, except earlier version of the inns, was here in the days of the coach traveller. This area was Charlton Heath, leading into Woolwich Common, open country with wide views back to London and across the Thames. It was also a dangerous area to cross, even more infested with highway robbers of all kinds than was Blackheath.

As with Deptford and Greenwich, the Dover Road avoids the important Thames-side town of Woolwich, the location of royal dockyards since the time of Henry VIII. The parishioners around the open heathland, which lies between fifty and seventy metres about sea level, had historic rights of pasturage for their animals and turbary (turf-cutting) and the right to cut furze for fuel. There was also gravel extraction.

From the late 18th century military purposes began to encroach on the common land as the Board of Ordnance bought more and more of it and barracks and exercise grounds were built.

The route begins to climb steeply, rising up Shooters Hill

which is still partly open country today, although this is difficult to see from the modern road. The gibbeted bodies of executed felons would be found all along the way, and on 11th April 1661 Samuel Pepys wrote of a journey home from Rochester, '...[I] rode under the man that hangs upon Shooters Hill; and a filthy sight it was to see how his flesh is shrunk to his bones.' The last execution here was in 1805.

The first turning on the right after the junction with the A205 leads to Severndroog Castle, a folly tower begun in 1784 to commemorate Commodore Sir William James on the orders of his widow. In 1755 Sir William had destroyed the Maratha Empire's island fortress of Suvarnadurg (corrupted in English into Severndroog) on the western coast of India, between Mumbai and Goa. It can be visited, but best to check the opening times first. (www.severndroogcastle.org.uk)

Just before the very crest of the hill is the rebuilt *Bull Inn* on the left (*8 miles*). This was the first post-house for a change of horses after London. It was also reputed to be the inn where Dick Turpin – the real one who was a thoroughly unpleasant thug and nothing like the romantic hero of legend – held the landlady over the fire to force her to reveal where her money was hidden. It would certainly have provided rich pickings for him as *The Bull* was patronised by many wealthy travellers.

William Hickey records in his memoirs published in 1761 that a gentleman, hearing that he wanted to lay on a truly extravagant dinner party, said to him, '...let me recommend to you to employ Logon, of the Bull upon Shooter's hill, which is out and out the most extravagant tavern in all England, where, however, you will be served in a princely style, and find every article of the very best.' Hickey inspected the inn and the landlord '...then conducted us into a noble room, magnificently furnished, which he said had been fitted up only three months before, and was intended for an assembly established by the principal families for twenty miles round the country. There were two spacious rooms adjoining the large one for cards, and a suite of supper rooms below.'

Despite the horrors of highwaymen and their corpses there was also a small spa industry at this point. John Evelyn records taking the waters there in 1699 and Queen Anne also drank them.

At the summit of the hill (132 metres) there was a signal beacon in the 16th century and a telegraph tower during the French and Napoleonic wars. After the top is reached the road descends steeply again, down through a patch of open country into Welling, passing on the left the little triangular piece of common, Shoulder of Mutton Green. (*9¼ miles*). Welling (*10 miles*) is an Anglo-Saxon place name but coachmen, who liked to spin tall tales, would tell passengers that it was really Well-End, meaning the safe deliverance from the perils of Shooters Hill.

The road would have been running through open farmland now, but passengers would have noticed Danson Park lying to the south of the road halfway between Shoulder of Mutton Green and Crayford. Within the park is Palladian villa designed by Sir Robert Taylor (architect of the Bank of England) for Sir John Boyd.

The modern road now runs through Bexley Heath, solidly built up with the original village of Bexley to the south and

Crayford to the east. Until the 1817 enclosure this was completely open common land and heath and ran down a long hill into the little town of Crayford. (*13 miles*)

Crayford to Greenhithe

Enter Crayford on A207. At roundabout with B2174 continue straight on to A226 (Dartford Road becoming West Hill) to enter Dartford. At roundabout with A2018 continue straight on to A226 (West Hill). Continue on A226 one-way system bypassing town centre. (To visit town centre keep to the right after the roundabout and at the traffic lights turn right following signs for Priory Centre parking.) Continue on A226 (East Hill becoming The Brent.) At the roundabout with the A2500 continue on the A226 (The Brent becoming London Road.)

*

Crayford was the place where the Jutish invaders are supposed to have won a great victory over the Britons in AD457. It was a flourishing industrial town from the 16th century when there was iron working, linen-bleaching and, later, textile printing. By the beginning of the 20th century, it had, 'I fear, no attraction whatever,' according to Charles G. Harper. Many of the historic buildings were demolished in the 1930s and wartime bombing took out most of the rest, leaving only the Norman church of St Paulinus.

The coaches stopped at the long-vanished *White Swan* and would then have crossed the River Cray (*13 ¼ miles*) which the road still does, just at the junction with the A2000.

Dartford, however, has kept a tiny portion of its old centre along with its premier coaching inn, *The Bull* (*14 ¾ miles*). Coaches from London had a steep hill down to contend with (West Hill) then a steep hill out (East Hill), both the scene of numerous accidents until the turnpike trust made cuttings through the highest points in 1820. A gate 'for the receipt of Post Horse tickets' (Cary) was located at the top of West Hill.

To see anything of the old town it is necessary to park in the Priory multi-storey and walk up to Spital Street, turning right to find *The Bull* (now *The Royal Victoria and Bull Hotel*) on the corner, just at the start of the pedestrianised section.

There has been an inn on this site since 1360, with a flourishing trade serving pilgrims on their way to Canterbury. Its original name was *The Holly Bull*, a corruption of Holy Bull, as the name refers to a papal seal (bulla), not to the animal. The present building dates from 1703 and retains its galleried inn yard, now with a glass roof.

In September 1790 John Byng stayed here at the end of a journey through Kent. 'Here [Dartford] at one of the miserable inns (the Bull), did I put up and with difficulty made retire two men who were introduced into my room [private parlour]; nor was Pony much happier in his miserable stable. Here every minute seem'd an hour…'

Continuing along the pedestrianised street towards the church there are remnants of Dartford's old houses. Holy Trinity is a Norman foundation much enlarged in the 13th century when a chapel to St Thomas à Becket was added. It retains a number of interesting monuments.

The River Darent in front of the church is now bridged by the A226. In medieval times this was a ford guarded by a hermit who had a cell in the church. The coaches would have rumbled over a bridge of 1461 until a new one was built in 1754, a long, low and rather attractive structure, now lost.

Leaving Dartford up East Hill there is a cemetery on the left at the roundabout and the road becomes The Brent. This was the beginning of the Brent or Burnt Heath, open country of which the cemetery, and playing fields and a park on the right hand side behind the houses, are the only remnants at this point. Here three Protestant martyrs were burned at the stake in 1555.

The next roundabout marks the point where, in the Middle Ages, the Dover Road left the line of Watling Street. The old Roman road is the more direct route but the main coaching traffic ran to Gravesend, closer to the Thames.

The road continues uphill to Stone, now a suburban sprawl, then passes few a scattered dwellings on the sandy heathland, pock-marked with quarries and lined with the walls of quarries on the northern side and houses on the southern. We are on high ground here, as rare glimpses northwards reveal. At 16 miles was John's Hole toll gate (presumably at the site of an early pit) and then the little village of Stone with *The King's Head* public house and the Stone toll gate, where a ticket would take you on past Chalk Street.

Now the road runs through modern Greenhithe, but in coaching days the town did not reach out this far and the coaches passed it by. With the exception of Stone, and scattered hamlets and farms, the road from Dartford ran through open country to Northfleet.

Greenhithe to Strood

Continue on A226 into Northfleet, then B2175 (High Street) to The Hill. After the tall brick tower of the Roman Catholic church take second right onto B261 (Dover Road becoming Old Road West, then Old Road East) to rejoin A226. Continue to Strood, joining A2, becoming High Street, and cross the bridge.

*

Northfleet, a bustling ship-building town with flint and chalk quarries, must have been a welcome sight after the dreary heath. The main inn was *The Queen's Head* (*20 miles*) on The Hill, the point where the road begins to climb in earnest out of the town. It was rebuilt in 1909 in black and white half-timbered style and is now a restaurant.

At the very end of the coaching era, in the 1830s, Jeremiah Rosher had the idea of developing a new town – Rosherville – between Northfleet and Gravesend. The town never happened, but he built a pier for the steam boat day trippers and a pleasure garden that was a huge success for its bands, promenades and famous shrimp and watercress teas.

Commercial watercress production began in this area in 1808 when William Bradbury of Springhead near Gravesend began to cultivate a ditch-weed by laying out beds. He produced such a good crop that he was soon able to establish a London market for it. He made a fortune and travellers were offered watercress at all the inns in the area.

Early coaches would have passed through Gravesend, an exceedingly busy centre for river traffic to and from London, but by 1787 it had been effectively by-passed by a new turnpike road (now B261) and the road books do not mention inns or give much information for the town.

The new road ran uphill to Chalk Street (*23 miles*) where there was a toll gate, just about where the B261 joins the A226. The ticket purchased at Stone would allow you free passage here.

Chalk itself was a tiny village of scattered houses and from there the road ran in easy undulations through open countryside. The Halfway Garage, just before the turning to Shorne, is a reminder that there used to be at least two roadside inns hereabouts calling themselves 'halfway houses'. Although there is little to see now, in coaching days there was a straggle of houses at this point and *The Crown* public house (*25 miles*).

There is a very gentle ascent to Gad's Hill (*26 miles*), famous later in the 19th century as the location of Charles Dicken's home. Gad's Hill's scatter of cottages have been overwhelmed now by the village of Higham on the northern side of the road, but this was once dense woodland, perilous for travellers. Shakespeare has Falstaff and Prince Hall dress up as highway robbers to frighten passers-by at Gad's Hill and the Danish Ambassador was set upon and robbed here in 1656.

Even worse, in October 1661 Prince Cossuma Albertus of Transylvania, on a diplomatic mission to Charles II, was stranded on Gad's Hill when his carriage became stuck in the terrible mud and potholes. As he slept he was stabbed to death by his coachman, Isaac Jacobs who, in league with the footman, dumped the decapitated body in a ditch and made off with the Prince's possessions. Both were hanged and Jacob's body gibbeted on Gad's Hill. The Prince was buried in Rochester Cathedral.

In 1676 a robbery here was the origin of the legend of Dick Turpin's epic ride to York on Black Bess. However, the real journey was nothing to do with that unpleasant thug but was carried out by William Neverson, known as Master Nicks, and later dubbed Swiftnicks by Charles II. At four in the morning he robbed a gentleman on Gad's Hill and rode off at high speed (on a bay horse, not a black one), arriving in York that afternoon. He found the Lord Mayor was playing bowls with a party of tradesmen, joined them and fixed the time of his arrival in their minds by making a bet on the game.

When Swiftnicks was eventually arrested he called the Lord Mayor as a witness to his alibi and was acquitted. Once safe, he admitted that he had done the deed but, having been found innocent, there was nothing to be done. He eventually met his end on the gallows in 1685.

Stories of this kind were the stock in trade of both coachmen and guards who would keep passengers entertained with them in the hope of increasing their tips at the end of the journey.

Dickens bought Gad's Hill Place (on the right of the road) from Mrs Eliza Lynn Linton (1822-98), the first salaried female journalist. When she lived there as a child the stages were still running and she remembered, 'Ninety-two public coaches and pleasure-vans used to pass in the day, not counting the private carriages of the grandees posting luxuriously to Dover for Paris and the grand tour. Soldiers marching or riding to or from Chatham and Gravesend to embark for India…ship's companies paid off that morning…gypsies and travelling tinkers…and sturdy beggars…'

On the opposite side of the road to the Place is the *Sir John Falstaff* inn, built in the late 17th century. In September 1790 John Byng noted, '…we took our way to Gad's Hill, to the public house, Sir John Falstaff, where, entering a good parlour, I made my breakfast with two travellers enjoying the view and the early morning.'

From here the road runs downhill all the way to Strood (*28 miles*) where there was a toll gate before the Medway bridge. This is open country for much of the way now, as it was in coaching days, although appreciating the landscape is difficult with the road so much widened and with major junctions.

In 1895 Charles G Harper described Strood as, '..one long street of miscellaneous houses with fields and meadows running up to the back yards; with engine-shops, mills, wheelwrights and a variety of other noisy trades clanging and clattering at the rear and an old church on the hillside to the left, appropriately dedicated to that patron of thieves and sailor-men, Saint Nicholas.' That church was designed by Sir Robert Smirke and opened in 1814 and is one of the few buildings left in the High Street that recall earlier times.

Where the Medway runs into the Thames it is wide enough for the major dockyard at Chatham to operate and to allow the Dutch fleet to sail in and do significant damage in the 17th century. Bridging the distance – about 170 metres or 570 feet – over tidal waters must have been difficult in the medieval period but there was a wooden bridge that, in 1391, was replaced by a stone structure with eleven arches. (*29 miles*). To maintain it there were endowments of land from Henry IV and Henry V as well as other local benefactors. Funds must have been ample and maintenance thorough, because it was still in operation in 1824 when it was widened.

In 1697 intrepid traveller Celia Fiennes travelled the Dover road at a time before the turnpikes made travel easier and safer, and described the Medway and the bridge. (The spelling is hers.) '..the Medway, which is the finest River I ever saw it runs thence to the sea and meets the Thames at the Boy [buoy] in Nore and so they fall into the sea together, but it ebbs and flows up a great way above Rochester and is very salt; the Bridg at Rochester is the finest in England, nay its said to equal any in the world, it is not built upon with houses as London Bridge, but its very long and fine iron spikes like a grate is on the top of the wall which is breast high...' She noted that there was a drawbridge between two of the arches to allow shipping to pass.

All the coaching traffic would have crossed over this bridge and it continued in use until 1856 when it was demolished, not because it was in bad condition but to allow larger shipping to pass through a new swing bridge. After several alterations, and the addition of a second roadway in 1970, there is now effectively a double bridge.

Rochester to Sittingbourne

Continue on the A2, unless stopping to visit. To visit the town centre and High Street it will be necessary to park: either take the A2 (Corporation Street) to the Corporation Street multi-storey car park or turn right immediately after the bridge and follow signs to the Bodley Hill car park (for the castle) or the other central car parks. On leaving, take Chatham High Street to its end and rejoin A2. Continue on A2 to Sittingbourne, taking the ring-road around the pedestrianised centre. Leave on the A2.

*

Rochester High Street is long, narrow and retains a significant number of old houses and inns. It is so narrow, and was always so busy, that negotiating it in any kind of vehicle must have been exceedingly difficult and it is no surprise that it is pedestrianised today.

The imposing keep of the castle (a 'pretty little thing' according to Celia Fiennes) was built in 1127 and survived a lengthy siege by King John to remain an actively garrisoned fortress until the 16th century. The cathedral, founded in AD 604, is the second oldest in the country after Canterbury. The present building was created in 1080. Much Norman work remains but there are also fine medieval sections.

The inns recommended in the road books were *The Bull, The Crown* and *The Old King's Head. The Bull* is now *The Royal Victoria and Bull Hotel* (16-18, High Street) and claims to be over four hundred years old. The website http://www.dover-kent.com/2014-project/Bull-Inn-Rochester.html has some fascinating early images and news items about the inn. It is also mentioned in the Pickwick Papers and in 1836 Queen Victoria, then a young princess, stayed there.

The Crown, rebuilt in Victorian times, is immediately ahead and to the right as you leave the bridge. *The Old King's Head* is now just *The King's Head* and presents an 18th century front at 58, High Street. It may well be older and looks it from the side. All these pubs have origins in the middle ages.

Even on Cary's map of 1794, Chatham and Rochester merge. Rochester's High Street becomes East Gate and then, at the point where the A2 meets it, Chatham High Street begins. Chatham's High Street (*30 miles*) is wider and less picturesque than Rochester's, but a good many Georgian and earlier buildings remain along its considerable length.

As well as the two miles of dockyards – Celia Fiennes saw two docks for building ships and others for refitting – that stretched away to the north, there was a large military presence at Chatham, stationed in Fort Pitt to the south. There were barracks, military hospitals, workshops, stores and parade grounds throughout the area. At noon a midday gun would be fired from Fort Pitt, at the sound of which the local boys used to throw themselves to the ground as though shot as a joke on passing strangers.

The atmosphere for the traveller must have been very different from that of Rochester with its more cultural attractions of cathedral and historic castle which might have tempted them to break their journey. Here the lanes and alleys running off the High

Street were crowded and disreputable, full of cheap lodging houses and little workshops.

The picture *Paid off at Chatham* by R. Deighton shows a late 18th century scene with cheerful sailors who have just received their pay being greeted by various 'ladies of the town'. In the background their shipmates are piling onto the roof of a very overcrowded stagecoach, clearly the worse for drink and waving bottles in the air.

The Mitre and *The Sun* were the two principal inns which have both been demolished and not rebuilt. *The Mitre* was in what is now the pedestrianised eastern end of the High Street at number 198 and *The Sun* was at 85, High Street.

After Chatham there was a stretch of open country devoted to cherry and apple orchards before the village of Rainham (*34 miles*) was reached. The ancient church of St Helen and St Giles was begun in about 1170 and still retains many Norman features. The village's inns gained a considerable income in the summer as a destination for local revellers, mainly from Chatham, but none of them are listed in the road books, presumably because changes of horse were made at Rochester and Chatham.

The low-lying land to the north of the road to the Medway was marshy and this was one of the parts of Kent that was considered to have 'wealth without health' because of the agues, fevers and breathing problems that arose from the wetlands.

Just a field separates the end of Rainham's High Street from the hamlet of Moor Street (*34 ½ miles*) where the road begins a long, gentle climb up Hartlip Hill. Newington (*36 ¾ miles*) stands on ground high enough to be free of the bad effects of the marshes. It is still a village and retains its old inn, *The Bull*, on the right hand side of the High Street. The church is a distance outside the village, which may have disappointed the passengers intrigued by tales of the Devil's footprints in the churchyard wall.

This was still cherry orchard country, with the trees interspersed with lush meadows full of sheep. Celia Fiennes wrote, 'Thence to Sittingburn all in sight of the lovely Medway.' The road climbs the long, gentle Keycol Hill before descending again into the valley where Key Street (*38 miles*) stands at the junction with the road between Maidstone and Sheerness (now A249).

Once across the roundabout the urban sprawl of Sittingbourne begins, but in coaching days there was open country for another mile to the hamlet of Chalk Well (*39 miles*).

From there it was less than a mile to Sittingbourne (*39¼ miles*). Although it was on the main route it was, until 1800, much less important than Milton Regis, a village just to its north. Milton Regis was an early Medieval port and royal borough, but when a combination of the silting of its creek and flooding of the marshes closed the port it sank into a slow decline while Sittingbourne, on the main road, began to prosper.

In 1798, Milton was described by Edward Hasted (*History and Topographical Survey of the County of Kent*) as '...[not] in any degree pleasant, the narrow streets, or rather lanes in it, being badly paved, and for the most part inhabited by seafaring persons, fishermen, and oyster-dredgers'. Today it retains many old buildings along its High Street and makes a picturesque detour.

Sittingbourne '...is a very good town for the road and travellers as you shall meete with, the church is all built with flints headed so curiously that it looks like glass and shines with the suns reflection.' (Celia Fiennes)

It had a post office and two principle inns, *The Rose* and *The George*. *The Rose* at 50, High Street was described by Hasted as 'the principal inn now in it [Sittingbourne], called the Rose... perhaps the most superb of any throughout the kingdom and the entertainment afforded in it equally so.' This makes it seem even worse that it has been hacked about on the ground floor (by the late 19th century it was a grocer's shop) and at the time of writing houses an eyesore Poundland store. What it looked like in its heyday can been seen here http://www.dover-kent.com/2014-project-a/Rose-Inn-Sittingbourne.html.

In September 1790 John Byng. '...dined very comfortably at the Rose Inn. The apartments are good, but the stabling very bad.'

The much smaller, and older, *George* is still a pub at 41, High Street. In 1815 *The George* alone kept forty pairs of post-horses which, given that the High Street was lined with other inns and posting houses, gives some indication of how busy the town was. The principal early inn was *The Red Lion*, now rebuilt. In 1415 this was one of the places where Henry V stayed on his way back to London from the battle of Agincourt and Henry VIII stayed while on progress in 1541.

The main industries of Sittingbourne by the beginning of the 20th century were brick, tile and paper making but in coaching days about three quarters of the inhabitants made their living in some way by servicing travellers – inn keepers, ostlers, post-boys, inn staff, farriers, blacksmiths and so on. The coming of the railways must have been a serious economic blow. As Charles G. Harper put it, 'When the railway came ruin, swift and terrible, fell upon this busy community. Grass grew in the stable-yards; the old high-hung yellow chariots and the light post-chaises rotted to pieces...'

There are numerous old buildings left' but as the High Street is partly pedestrianised now it is necessary to park the car and explore on foot.

Sittingbourne to Canterbury

Leave on the A2. After the roundabout with A299 take the first on the left signposted Boughton and Dunkirk. Continue through Boughton Street and Boughton under Blean (The Street becoming Canterbury Road) and Dunkirk and rejoin A2. Take next slip-road to left after service station, signposted to Upper Hambledon and Chartham (London Road becoming Roman Road) Turn left onto A2050 and immediately right, signposted Harbledon. (Faulkners Lane becoming Church Hill then Summer Hill). Go under A2050 to roundabout and take first exit (London Road) into Canterbury. At T-junction by St Dunstan's church turn right onto A290 (St Dunstan's Street) to Westgate Tower.

*

As now, the road ran on from Sittingbourne through open farmland, past hop gardens and orchards. Celia Fiennes wrote, 'Thence to Canterbury, we pass by great Hopyards on both sides of the Road and this year was great quantities of fruite here in

106

Kent.' The road passes through the hamlets of Bapchild (from the Old English for Bacca's Spring), Radfield and tiny Green Street (*44 ½ miles*) (now on the maps as Teynham) with *The Swan Inn* (now rebuilt).

The modern traveller arrives in Faversham next, but in coaching days the town lay to the north of the Dover road and Ospringe (*46 miles*) and the now vanished Red Lion – 'A tolerable inn' according to Hasted – was the place to change horses.

Ospringe has a very fine monument to the medieval pilgrims in the Maison Dieu, endowed by Henry III in 1234. The foundation was staffed by a master, three brethren of the Order of the Holy Cross and two secular clerks, who celebrated mass for the soul of the king and his family. They were also required to succour passers-by and pilgrims and to keep the *Camera Regis*, or the king's chamber, for when a monarch travelled this way. The Maison Dieu is now in the care of English Heritage and can be visited at certain times.

Farmland, orchards and small hamlets continued to Boughton Street (*49 miles*) and Boughton Hill (*50 miles*). This was, and still is, soft fruit and hop-country. Well into the 20th century hop-pickers would travel from the East End of London for a working holiday in the hop-gardens, camping out or living in rough huts erected by the hop growers.

Boughton-under-Blean is described by Charles G. Harper as, 'perhaps the neatest, quietest, longest, and most cheerfully picturesque village on the Dover Road.' The road rises steadily uphill all the way until it reaches a plateau of woodland, pasture and moor, the ancient Forest of Blean. It would have been a long, hard pull for the horses.

The road leads on to Dunkirk whose name is explained by Halsted who says the dwellings there were 'inhabited by low persons of suspicious character, this being a place exempt from the jurisdiction of either hundred or parish, as in a free port, which receives all who enter it, without distinction. The whole district from hence gained the name of Dunkirk.' Because there was no parish jurisdiction, the road was in particularly bad repair here until it was turnpiked late in the 18th century.

From this height there was a view for pilgrims of the cathedral ahead as they stopped at the Harbledown toll gate (*52 ½ miles*) and perhaps had time for a quick drink at *The Gate Inn.*

After that the road swoops in a series of switchbacks that must have put a strain on the horses, especially the wheelers who took most of the effort of braking a coach. It goes through the little village of Upper Harbledown, then makes a long descent into the valley of the River Stour through Harbledown. The switchback nature of the road is so pronounced that Chaucer describes Harbledown as '…a little town Which that yelped [is called] Bob-up-and-doun, Under the Blee in Canterbury way.'

Blee is an alternative spelling of Blea or Blean, the high area of ancient woodland and rough common the road has skirted from Boughton to this point.

The road plunges down into Harbledown to a bend in the road, then climbs up again between high banks. Perched on either side are not one, but two, ancient churches. On the left as you ascend is the parish church of St Michael and All Angels (*54 miles*). It is a very simple early Norman church which has been much altered and added to over the years.

On the other side of the road is the Church and Hospital of St Nicholas. It was founded in about 1064 by Archbishop Lanfranc as a leper hospital and may have been the first in this country. Lepers would beg for alms from passersby and would offer prayers for the souls of benefactors. It is known that Henry II called here as he made his penitential journey to Canterbury to atone for the murder of Thomas à Becket. By about 1400 the scourge of leprosy had subsided, for reasons that are not fully understood, and the hospital became alms houses. That use has continued up to the present, although the range of dwellings was rebuilt in 1840.

Begging for alms continued after the lepers had departed. In 1512 the scholar Erasmus and Dean Colet, founder of St Paul's School, returned this way from Canterbury and were confronted by an elderly man who sprinkled them with holy water and proffered what purported to be a shoe belonging to St Thomas to be kissed. Dean Colet was angry: 'What! Do these asses expect us to kiss the shoes of all good men who have ever lived?' but apparently Erasmus gave the man a coin.

The grounds are private, but it is possible to walk around the very attractive gardens with their view down to Canterbury.

Church Hill reaches its summit, becomes Summer Hill, then descends to the valley bottom where it passes under the modern A2050, carrying traffic straight to the ring road around the historic centre of Canterbury. Like the pilgrims and later travellers we can follow the original road into the suburb of St Dunstan's and approach the city as they would have done.

Canterbury

At the T-junction by St Dunstan's church turn right onto St Dunstan's Street (A290) to the roundabout in front of Westgate Towers. Parking is difficult and expensive: For Park & Ride leave the ring road on the A2050 towards Dover and follow the signs.

*

St Dunstan's church is the burial place of the head of Sir Thomas More, rescued by his daughter Margaret after his execution and placed here in the family vault of her husband's family, the Ropers. Rather earlier, in 1174, this was the place where Henry II changed into sackcloth and walked barefoot to the cathedral to do penance for the murder of Thomas à Becket.

Canterbury's ancient walls still partly ring the city and coaches would have crossed the River Stour and entered through West Gate as we still can. (*55¼ miles*) It is the only survivor of the seven medieval gates, protected, perhaps by the fact that it was a debtors' prison.

'...it's a noble Citty, the gates are high tho' but narrow, the streets are most of them large and long and the buildings handsome, very neat but not lofty, most are of brickwork; it's a flourishing town, good trading in the Weaving of Silks.' Celia Fiennes also observed water-powered paper mills and crowds of people who had come to the area for hop picking.

The cathedral – 'the finest sight there' – is the oldest in England and travellers often stopped for sightseeing, even if they were not strictly pilgrims. Celia Fiennes admired the carving, the stained glass and the Chapter House, viewed the effigy of the Black Prince and noted that the crypt had been given to the French Protestants for worship. Presumably these were Huguenot refugee silk weavers.

John Byng, '...made my wander by the old walls and gates of this old and much-worthy-of-observation town.' He admired the castle, 'a curious old magnificent ruin' and was dragged around the cathedral by a guide, '...a boy in full ignorant prate.' He was less admiring of the interior than Celia Fiennes – 'The screen and painted windows would yet do honour to the Popish Faith, and might raise a sigh over the Ruins of Religion!'

Horses would be changed at Canterbury and Cary's *New Itinerary* names only three Canterbury inns, although the city was packed with them. In 1686 a survey found beds for 236 travellers and stabling for 436 horses.

The best located inn must have been *The Red Lion* which was demolished in 1806 when Guildhall Street was created. It stood on the corner of High Street and Guildhall Street where there is currently a Costa coffee shop. It was an ancient inn and entertained the ambassadors of Emperor Charles V in 1520. In 1762 the French Duc de Nivernais, sent by Louis XV to negotiate the end of the Seven Years' War, stayed there, exhausted with sea and coach sickness. He was presented with a dinner bill for £44 10s 8d. The next night in Rochester he ate for 3 guineas. The news of the extortionate bill got out and such was the bad feeling against the landlord that he was bankrupted within six months.

The King's Head in Wincheap Street advertises itself as the oldest functioning pub in Canterbury and is in the records from 1692. The building is undoubtedly older than that, but this inn was well outside the city walls and unlikely to have attracted as much business as the central ones. However, this was the lodging chosen by John Byng who had come to Canterbury on the Maidstone road. From that direction Wincheap would have been the obvious stopping place.

He did not think much of *The King's Head*. 'Here lodged…in a great parlour… Canterbury is much improved by the new paving, but the inns are wretched. Whitings and… mackerel served for the chief of my supper, whilst the Colonel ate away at Whitstable oysters.' He did report a 'tolerable dinner' the second night, rose at seven the next morning and '…cross'd the street to a barber's shop and there shaved and dressed myself. After waiting some time for breakfast and a hot roll, I was glad to get away…'

The Fountain (later *The Royal Fountain Hotel*) in St Margaret's Street was destroyed in 1942 by German bombs. It stood just off the High Street and it seems strange now that it was on a side street. However, coaches would have turned off the High Street, travelled down St Margaret's Street and then left onto Watling Street and followed it out onto the Old Dover Road. The modern road runs parallel but to the northeast of it.

The old and new roads join up at what was the Gutteridge Gate (*57 miles*), now marked by the *Old Gate* pub and the location of the Park and Ride. The P&R bus goes into the city along the route of the Old Dover Road and returns on the modern road.

Gutteridge Gate to Dover

Continue on A2050, cross the A2, go through Bridge and join the A2 until right turn for Lydden (signposted Lydden and Temple Ewell). Follow Lydden Hill into Lydden, becoming Canterbury Road, then London Road into Temple Ewell. Continue on London Road to roundabout, take 2nd exit onto A256 (London Road) signposted Dover Town Centre. Continue on A256 into Dover. It is easier to park and explore on foot.

*

Charles G. Harper describes the sixteen miles that remain to Dover as passing over 'bare and exposed downs, with here and there a little village nestling, sheltered from the bleak winds, in deep valleys.' For some reason the stretch between Canterbury and Barham Downs was not turnpiked until the 1780s. Celia Fiennes commented, '…and so to Dover, much up hill and down, it was a good road and sort of champion country, yet at a distance you see many good woods and pretty houses with rows of trees.'

The first village is Bridge (*58¼ miles*) named for the crossing of the Nail Bourne which eventually, well to the north, becomes the Lesser Stour. By-passed by the modern road it retains some charm. The road continues over Barham Downs and chalk downland to Lydden (*65½ miles*), a long run without much in the way of shelter in case of accident or bad weather.

Lydden lies folded deep in one of the dry valleys that are a feature of the downs and the road to it is a very long hill down to the village pond and *The Bell* inn. No sooner has the road reached the village before it climbs out of the valley again towards Temple Ewell (*67½ miles*) where springs produce the River Dour that runs down into Dover. Here was the last toll gate before the port.

The Dour was managed from a very early date, both for industry – corn and paper mills – and for landscaping around the grounds of what used to be the Abbey. The hamlet of Crabble with another corn mill, open to the public, lies to the right hand side of the road. The 69 milestone stood just about where modern Pilgrim's Way comes in from the left.

The road runs steadily downhill. This was still open countryside for coach travellers but today is covered by the outskirts of Dover. In the village of Buckland the road divided and the Dover road went slightly to the right and then continued downhill. Now this is one-way running north and to drive it necessitates going into Dover and then back out.

The old road continued down this right fork, Buckland Road, which became London Street, then High Street. Gradually the slope lessens until the road reached, on the left, the Maison Dieu, the town hall since 1834. It was founded in 1203 to accommodate pilgrims from the Continent travelling to the shrine of Thomas à Becket in Canterbury. Parts of the medieval building remain and it was restored in the last quarter of the 19th century.

At this point the road divided and the Folkestone road went off to the right. Dover traffic would have continued down the now-pedestrianised Biggin Street which becomes Cannon Street before reaching the Market Place (*71 miles*). This probably where passengers who were not intending to take a ship across to France would have disembarked.

In the Market Place *The Bull* had a large assembly room for balls and concerts, *The City of Antwerp* was a substantial inn, while *The Walmer Castle* was rather smaller. Numerous inns, taverns and small hotels were located throughout Dover but the ones mentioned in the road books were all located in the harbour to be convenient for the ships.

Now it is impossible to even view the streets where these harbourside inns and hotels stood, because the A20 runs right along the waterfront and, with war-time bombing and the expansion of the docks and ferry facilities, completely obliterated them. To gain an approximate idea of the location, they all faced onto the southernmost dock basins where the marina and lifeboat station are located.

The Ship was the premier Dover inn and stood on Custom House Quay. The frontage was wide with semi-circular sections at each end and six windows across between them. It had three main floors and a full-width balcony. Byron, probably referring to *The Ship*, wrote of the 'long, long bills, whence nothing is deducted.'

As well as the London stages it was also a stopping point for more local services.

"A STAGE COACH sets off every Monday and Friday from the Ship Inn, Dover at 6 o'clock in the morning for Margate; calls for passengers and parcels at the "Three Kings" Deal at half past seven; the "Bell" Sandwich at nine; the "Red Lion" Ramsgate at half past ten; stops at Mitchener's, Margate, three hours and returns the same road to Dover in the evening. William HARRISON."

The York House was not quite as smart as *The Ship* which was opposite it, but in 1797 the Duke of Clarence, later William IV, stayed there. One assumes the landlord treated his monarch better than he did John Byng, when he stayed there in 1790. As usual, he was not reticent about expressing his opinions. '... the York Hotel where amidst noise and racket, we procured a mean dirty parlour for ourselves, and a kind of shiphold for our horses. Bad specimen this to the French, of English comforts! Bread and wine not to be endured; with a nasty brown fricassee and old tough partridges! A room full of wind and ships' stinks!!' The next day, 'Our dinner was ill served and [as] nasty as possible, with not-drinkable wine! We had to endure a tedious evening, from the want of good apartments and good cheer.'

The next day he wrote, 'Never did I enter a more dirty, noisy or more imposing [ie they were imposed upon, it was very expensive] inn as this York House.'

In 1836 the *Phoenix* coach left the hotel at seven a.m. daily to *The George* and *The Blue Boar* in Holborn. The fare was £1.

The City of London was in the harbour area but slightly back from the waterside with entrances on both Council House Street and Round Tower Street (both now vanished). The *Eagle* coach started from here. It was destroyed by fire in 1810 but rebuilt. *The Royal Hotel* was in Snargate Street which ran along under what is now the A20 for some distance.

During the French wars commercial shipping across to the Continent was severely hampered, both by privateering and by government prohibitions. The official packet boats that carried the posts were transferred to Harwich, but the owners of the local packet boats, all from banking families, began flying the neutral Belgian flag and advertised that they were 'free from molestation from ships and privateers of the Powers at War.'

With the end of the Napoleonic Wars the packet service was officially resumed on 10 October 1815 and the size of the sloops was increased so the crossing was usually by vessels of 60 to 70 tons. If wind and tide were right passengers could land in Calais in as little as three hours, but if not it could take very much longer and passengers would arrive seasick, cold and often wet. It is unlikely that anyone travelling on the Dover coach to take the packet boat looked forward to the experience with any enthusiasm.

It was not unknown for passengers to suffer delays waiting for the tides and weather to be right for their ship to leave port. Despite the fact that the castle was a fully-garrisoned fortress it was possible to visit it, which must have made an interesting diversion. Celia Fiennes describes dropping a stone down the great well in the castle keep, '…which was a pretty time descending…[before] it plashed into the water.' The author tried exactly the same experiment.

The morning after John Byng arrived he and his companion took 'An early stroll upon the piers, where I saw two packet boats (with exiles, voluntary and involuntary) sail for Calais; also a King's Tender [naval supply boat]; and there was an Ostend East Indiaman lying off the harbour – many sailors employed in whiting-fishing.' After breakfast they walked on the beach and visited the new hot and cold salt-water baths – Dover was also a destination for seaside holidays – and climbed to the castle.

'It seemed necessary to have a cicerone about the castle [ie they found themselves with a guide to show them all the sights]... to fling stones into the well...and to peep into the old church, now a fives court.' The church is now restored and the Roman signal tower outside is still there.

'Descending the hill, we walk'd to the North end of the town to view the old ruin'd church, call'd Grace-Dieu, now converted into a King's Storehouse. [And now restored by the Victorians and used as the town hall.]...I strolled back thro' the town (observing a newly erected mischievous playhouse) and visited Mrs P. who formerly kept the inn called the City of London.' The next morning, before he left the town, Byng observed seven ships of the line passing down the Channel on the tide, including *The Victory* that was to become Nelson's flagship at the Battle of Trafalgar.

It seems that the traveller of the 17th, 18th and 19th centuries had as much to amuse them as the modern visitor – who has, hopefully, better lodgings.

The Brighton Road

Long before Brighton became a seaside resort in the 18th century, travellers were making their way down from London to the coast for trade, the transport of goods and for military purposes. As a result, from ancient times, there have always been a number of ways over the North and South Downs to the sea and the importance of each has varied with the development of better road surfaces and improved transport.

The 'Classic' Route from 1816

Southwark to the Elephant and Castle

Begin at London Bridge and follow the A3 Borough High Street south to the Elephant and Castle roundabout.

*

Before Westminster Bridge was built between 1739–1750 all traffic to the south of the river went via London Bridge, channelling trade through the City at the cost of huge congestion. As a result the Borough of Southwark on the south bank – usually simply referred to as Borough – developed a large number of inns to cater for coaches and waggons so they could unload passengers and goods to be taken on by lighter vehicles. The Dover Road section of this book has more information about Southwark.

Travellers to and from Brighton by the beginning of the 19th century would still have travelled through Southwark if they were coming to and from the City or the east and they would have found it as busy and commercially active as their medieval and Tudor counterparts did.

The traveller on the Brighton Road would have driven down the High Street and into Blackman Street which became the Newington Road. At the point where the Walworth Road went off to the south east, and the roads to the Thames led off west, there was an island of buildings in the centre of the junction with, at the northern tip, *The Elephant and Castle* inn. (*1 mile*). This is where, after 1819, travellers who had crossed by the new Southwark Bridge would have joined the route.

Westminster Bridge Variation

Begin at Westminster Bridge. Take Westminster Bridge Road A302 west to Elephant and Castle roundabout and join main route.

*

Westminster Bridge was the easiest route after 1750 for private carriages from the West End and for some coaches setting out from *The White Horse Cellar* in Piccadilly. Once over the Thames they would have driven along Westminster Bridge Road to the 'roundabout' formed around the obelisk at the centre of its junction with Great Surrey Street, Borough Road, Lambeth Road and London Road, then would have taken London Road (now St George's Road) to the south east and would have joined Newington Road in just over a quarter of a mile at what is now the Elephant and Castle roundabout. (*1 mile*)

Elephant and Castle to Kennington

Follow the A3 south on Newington Butts to Kennington Park Road and St Mark's church.

Now most famous for the Oval cricket ground, and close to Vauxhall Bridge (the original bridge was completed 1816), Kennington village was recorded in the Domesday Book and became part of the possessions of the Duchy of Cornwall.

Kennington Park on the eastern side of the road was, until 1851, an open common and a place of execution where, amongst others, minor prisoners from the 1745 Jacobite rebellion were hanged, drawn and quartered in 1746, while the more significant captives ended their days on the block at the Tower. Ironically, because Kennington was a royal manor, the Duke of Cumberland who had defeated the rebels was also Earl of Kennington. The last person to be executed on the common was a fraudster of the name of Badger in 1799.

The first of the two main variations to the Brighton road (the Sutton and Reigate route) occurs at what is now the cross road of the A3, the A202 and the A23. The main route continued south on the A23; the variation, described later, continues on the A3.

This was the point where the first of the nine tollgates on the Brighton road stood. It is illustrated vividly in James Pollard's print, *Kennington Gate - Derby Day* (1838) which can be easily found on-line. It was removed in October 1865. In the background of the image can be seen the tower of St Mark's church. (*1½ miles*)

Originally Kennington Common extended up to the site of the church and it was at this point that the Scottish rebels were executed and that highwaymen were executed and their bodies hung in the gibbet on public view. Jerry Abershawe was one of them, hanged here in 1795. The large Common was also the venue for fairs and bare-knuckle boxing matches which contributed to the area's reputation for riotous behaviour.

It also provided space for popular preachers. In 1739 George Whitefield. the radical Anglican clergyman and Methodist pioneer, preached nightly in the open air to crowds of between 30-50,000. Later that year, fellow Methodists John and Charles Wesley also preached regularly on the Common and attracted similar audiences. In the 1840s Kennington was the location for Chartist protest meetings.

The base of the gibbet was found when the foundations were dug for the church in 1824. The Greek revival-style church was one of the "Waterloo" churches built in south London with a contribution from a fund set up by the government as an act of commemoration for the defeat of Napoleon. There are four Waterloo churches in the area – an indication of the rapid growth of this part of London, with villages and hamlets being absorbed into one urban mass. There are still a number of terraces built in the late 18th and early 19th century, including some on Kennington Park Road, Cleaver Square and Kennington Road.

Kennington to Streatham

Fork left from A3 just before Kennington church onto A23 Brixton Road through Stockwell and Brixton on Brixton Hill, then Streatham Hill and Streatham High Road to Streatham.

*

As the street names reveal, the land is now beginning to rise steadily away from the Thames along the flank of Streatham Hill, following the line of a Roman road. Streatham is 'the hamlet on the street' and Brixton was 'Brixtane' or 'Brixstone' in Domesday Book, referring to the paved Roman way which still survived.

Stockwell was a little village surrounded by market gardens and the site of pioneer botanist John Tredescant's gardens in the 17th century. It was rapidly developed in the 19th century, merging into Brixton, but the 1816 map shows that the traveller would now have felt themselves in the open country and well clear of London.

Brixton itself was bounded on the eastern side by the River Effra running the short distance from the hills at Norwood to the Thames at Vauxhall. It has now vanished underground. Originally Brixton was a series of scattered hamlets – Brixton, Brixton Causeway (*2 miles*) and Brixton Hill – and was surrounded by open country, waste, marshy patches popular for wildfowl shooting, and common land which was enclosed in 1810.

The opening of Vauxhall Bridge in 1816 stimulated piecemeal development as the prosperous middle classes began to look for substantial and respectable suburban villas from which they could commute on the short-stage coach routes that developed to serve these areas. The traveller would have seen ribbon-development along the old lanes well before the market gardens and small fields were built over.

On Brixton Hill is St Matthew's church (*3 miles*). It is another Classical-style Waterloo church, consecrated in 1824 to serve the rapidly growing population. An indication of the gentrification of the area is the Budd family mausoleum which now stands out on the pavement in front of the church. It was erected by Richard Budd, a property developer and speculator in 1825 and commemorates his father Richard, 'of the Stock Exchange' as well as various other members of the family. The Budds, very much upper-middle class, lived in Russell Square and also had their own holiday home in Brighton, so they would have passed this monument on their regular trips to the seaside.

At the summit of the hill stands a windmill built in 1816. Very close is Brixton Prison which was opened in 1820 as Surrey House of Correction, situated in 'one of the most open and salubrious spots'.

The mill, which is the closest one to the centre of London that still survives, was converted to steam and gas in 1902 and continued to produce flour until 1934. It has been restored and is open to the public at certain times of the year.

At the 5 mile stone on Streatham Hill was the gibbet where the body of highwayman Jack Gutteridge was hanged in chains for the murder of a gentleman and his servant.

Streatham itself (5½ miles) is about halfway between London Bridge and Croydon where the Archbishops of Canterbury had a palace: the small Saxon settlement developed as a natural break-point in the archbishops' journeys. It grew with the discovery of mineral springs on the common in 1659 and people would travel out from London to take the waters.

By the beginning of the 18th century the spa was at its height, but although it attracted many fashionable visitors no-one seems to have thought of building accommodation and it fell into decline, closing in 1792. The dilapidated well-house and grounds, known as the Rookery, were eventually bought by the Council in 1912 and the house demolished, leaving only the gardens as a public open space at the eastern end of Streatham Common.

A second water source was found closer to the village centre and continued to pump and sell mineral water until the 1940s although, again, no-one capitalized on the spa by developing accommodation and other attractions. The well-house has been incorporated into a modern sheltered housing development.

Doctor Samuel Johnson was familiar with Streatham from frequent visits to long-vanished Streatham Place, owned by his great friend Mrs Hester Thrale. She would hold tea parties for such luminaries as Sir Joshua Reynolds, actor David Garrick and writer Fanny Burney, along with Doctor Johnson himself.

St Leonard's church was a fashionable place of worship, attended by all the Thrale's friends. The gentry went to St Leonard's while their servants worshipped at All Saints chapel of ease where the service started ten minutes later and finished ten minutes earlier than the one at the church, so their employers were not inconvenienced by their absence. When Doctor Johnson fell out with Mrs Thrale over her second marriage and left for the last time, he records visiting the church and kissing the porch in farewell. The church remains but was much restored and altered in 1831.

Streatham had a population of just under 3,000 in the first quarter of the 19th century, gradually swelling as more and more wealthy and fashionable people built country villas there. The short-stage commuter routes into London were well-used.

Streatham to Croydon

Continue on A23 London Road. At the one way system entering Croydon go straight on to A235 London Road which becomes the pedestrianised High Street. Turn right onto Tamworth Road. Park in this area to explore or continue to A236 Old Town.

*

Once out of the village of Streatham the traveller was in open country with only scattered hamlets. The area was infested with highwaymen and footpads in the 17th and 18th century, many of whom ended up on the large gallows near the hamlet of Norbury (*6¾ miles*). Norbury consisted of a scattering of buildings on the River Graveney from whose valley the land rose to Thornton Heath (*8 miles*) where charcoal burners worked and where robbers were just as much of a hazard.

To the east travellers can look towards the heights of Sydenham Hill (119 metres/390 feet) and South Norwood Hill (112 metres/367 feet). The roads south throughout this area cling to the flanks of hills and to valleys as the land rises steadily to the North Downs.

Thornton Heath hamlet had a horse-pond. It survives, much urbanised, in a large traffic island at the point where the A235 continues straight on into Croydon and the A23 swings off to by-pass it. It has now been drained, so even if a coach and four were to change horses here there would be no water for them to drink. Just before it is reached there is a turning to the left to Colliers'

Water Lane. About a mile and a half along it was Colliers' Water farmhouse, reputedly a haunt of Dick Turpin.

There was open country again before the town of Croydon was reached (*9 miles*), the first settlement of any significant size since leaving Southwark. Croydon lies where several dry valleys meet and this was the point where the Roman road from London to Portslade on the coast crossed the North Downs.

From the time of Domesday Book Croydon belonged to the Archbishops of Canterbury and they built a manor house, Croydon Palace, as a summer residence next to the parish church. It survives in part as the Old Palace of John Whitgift School and dates from at least the 12th century, although most of what remains today is from the 15th century and later.

The 15th century great hall is one of the finest surviving in southern England. Monarchs from Henry III to Elizabeth I banqueted there when they stayed at the palace and James I of Scotland spent time there when a prisoner in England after his capture in 1406.

West Croydon railway station is to your left as you turn onto Tamworth Road. This was the site of the great basin of the Croydon Canal which opened on 22nd October 1809. It ran from here to a junction with the Grand Surrey Canal and from there to the Thames via Forest Hill, Sydenham, and Anerley. However, it was a financial failure with the shares fetching just two shillings in 1830. The proprietors sold the canal to the new railway company and it closed in 1836. Only a few remnants are left, scattered along the route.

Croydon High Street, the route of the Brighton Road, is now pedestrianised and virtually nothing remains of the early 19th century or earlier, except the alms houses founded by Archbishop Whitgift in 1593 as the Hospital of the Holy Trinity. They still sit at the junction of North End, High Street, George Street and Church Street.

From the Middle Ages onwards Croydon was notorious for smoke from the charcoal burning industry. Charcoal was made from timber from the extensive forests of Sussex and Surrey and was sold to London between the 15th and 19th centuries until it was supplanted by sea-coal, shipped from Newcastle.

Modern Croydon lies on a ridge sloping down to the Old Town and the Wandle Valley, where the Roman road ran and the Palace and parish church are sited. A shift of the main route and the commercial centre seems to have occurred during the 18th century. As a result the modern traffic-flow south through the town reflects the very earliest route travellers would have taken while, by the time the Brighton Road was a specific entity, the higher High Street route would have carried the main traffic.

The High Street was widened in 1890 with a narrow escape for the Alms houses. This period also saw the disappearance of the main inns – *The Old King's Head*, once owned by John Ruskin's maternal grandmother, and *The Greyhound* which had a gallows sign right across the road, as did *The Crown*, opposite the Alms houses. *The Greyhound* was famous as the location of a major dispute during the Civil War between Cromwell and General Fairfax, who had his headquarters there in 1645.

Croydon to Merstham

Continue on the A236 Old Town out of Croydon. At the roundabout go straight on to A235 Brighton Road. Follow the one-way system through Purley to rejoin the A23 Brighton Road. Entering Coulsdon the modern road (Farthing Way) by-passes Coulsdon High Street, the original road. Continue on A23 and at the junction with M23 keep on A23 London Road North to Merstham High Street.

*

A glimpse of the Surrey Iron Railway would have been a novelty for coach travellers. This horse-drawn railway was begun in 1801 to provide a nine-mile-long link between Wandsworth on the Thames and the industries of the Wandle Valley via Tooting and Mitcham, with spurs off to various mills and works. It carried only freight – coal, building materials, lime, manure, corn and seeds – not passengers, and was operated by independent carriers using their own horses and wagons and paying tolls.

It was extended in 1805 through Purley and Coulsdon to quarries for limestone and fuller's earth near Merstham and the line of this track closely followed the road south of Croydon. It suffered from competition from the canal and later from the closure of the quarries and, of course, the arrival of the steam railway was the killer blow. It closed in 1846.

Coaches leaving Croydon would have encountered a toll gate at Hayling Park (*12 miles*) where *The Swan and Sugarloaf* inn (now a Tesco Express in the same late 19th century building) stands at the junction with the B275. Hayling Park lies to the right of the road just past the junction and is now the playing fields of Whitgift School.

The road curves through the valley alongside the railway to Purley. The coming of the railway created a modern town where before there was only a hamlet at the point where the Brighton Road and the routes south-east over the Downs divided. The junction with the A22 marks this fork, although there has been much disturbance to the road pattern. (*14½ miles*)

Travellers with an interest in politics would have been aware of Purley as the sometime home of John Horne Tooke, clergyman, pamphleteer, Member of Parliament and vociferous opponent of the American War. In 1777 he ended up in prison for describing the British attack on the colonists at Lexington as murder and he continued to agitate for the rest of his life.

Further south on the Brighton Road is modern Coulsdon. Old Coulsdon is to the south-east and this area was known as Smitham Bottom (*13½ miles*). Oddly, given the name, it is actually the top of a pass across the North Downs. At the end of the 19th century it was described as wind-swept, lonely and 'never beautiful'.

On 9th June 1788 there was a major bare knuckle boxing meeting here. According to *The Gentleman's and London Magazine: Or Monthly Chronologe* there were 'no less than three pitched battles fought' in a roped-off ring of twenty four feet in diameter with an inner area for 'gentlemen subscribers'. The gentlemen were rapidly displaced by a large and enthusiastic mob. The first fight was between Jackson and Fewterell – the first fight for the man who was to become the famous 'Gentleman' Jackson, the darling of Regency sporting gentlemen and friend of Byron and the Prince Regent. He won but not, apparently, impressively. The Prince Regent was present for the bout, accompanied by the Duke of Hamilton and Lord Melbourne.

With the coming of the railway the area developed rapidly, with no fewer than three stations within one mile, including the wonderfully-named Stoat's Nest. The new settlement was named Smitham (without the 'Bottom') and then became Coulsdon.

The main road now bypasses it and the only remnant of the coaching days, *The Red Lion* inn, has been demolished and is now under the car park of Aldi.

The road down to Merstham has been mangled by the junctions with the M23 and M25, but the curve by *The Feathers* hotel on entering the village is clear on the old maps. (*17¾ miles*)

Merstham had large greenstone quarries. In 1259 they were supplying stone for the Palace of Westminster and in 1801 a local boy called George Valentine Hall went to work in them. By the time that the new London Bridge was being built in 1824 his firm, Joliffe and Banks, were working on it and supplying stone from Merstham.

The main part of *The Feathers* was built in 1911 but it retains 18th century elements at the back and some of the outbuildings are 17th century. The toll gate stood just beyond it.

Merstham to Povey Cross

Leave Merstham on the A23, London Road South, to junction with A242, Gatton Park Road. Take the left hand fork on London Road to Redhill. At the Lombard roundabout approaching the town centre take the first exit, signposted Brighton. Continue following signs to A23 Brighton then follow A23 Brighton Road. Continue on A23 Horley Road through Earlswood, to Brighton Road through Salfords following A23 to Gatwick and Brighton. Follow Brighton Road through Horley to roundabout with A217. Take 2nd exit, Povey Cross Road. Past Airport Inn and Travelodge take first left following Povey Cross Road.

*

Gatton Park (*18½ miles*), on the right at the point where the A242 now forks off to the right, is a manorial parkland. In 1451 it was created a Parliamentary borough returning two Members of Parliament to represent a population that never numbered more than twenty voters. It was purchased by Sir Mark Gatton, a Scotsman who had a highly lucrative career with the East India Company, earning himself a fortune of over £200,000. He had been returned as Member for various rotten boroughs but after falling out with the Duchess of Newcastle in 1800 found himself without a patron. He bought Gatton for £95,000 and, as at the time every other property on the estate was occupied by tenants, he was the sole voter. He and his brother in law were duly elected to the two seats.

Gatton, along with many other 'rotten boroughs', lost its status in the 1832 First Reform Act, which must have been an unpleasant shock for Lord Monson who had bought the estate – and its seats – for £100,000 two years previously. It is difficult to feel much sympathy for a man who built a folly in front of Gatton Hall to represent the 'Town Hall' of the borough.

The road continues into what is now Redhill (*24 miles*). In 1816 when this became the most direct route to Brighton, by-passing Reigate, it was simply an area of common on top of a hill. There were two tan yards and a few cottages. What is now the town grew up as a result of the railway's arrival in the 1840s.

Redhill merges into Earlswood, another area that was originally a common. From here the road swept in a switchback through open country to the fork where the A23 goes right to Horley. Being so close to Gatwick airport the area is now solidly built-up. It used to be a marshy area watered by the tributaries of the River Mole with scattered farms and cottages and the church standing right to the south of the parish.

The Six Bells Inn (now *Ye Olde Six Bells* just in case someone doesn't recognize a genuinely old building when they see it) stands by the church in Church Road, just off the A23. The original Gatwick Farm, from which the airport was named, was just on the other side of the A23, opposite the church.

The old coaching route continued down what is now Povey Cross Road to where the road crossed the Mole at Kimberham Bridge (*26 miles*). The alternative route via Reigate joined this route at Povey Cross and continued south across Lowfield Heath, now completely covered by the airport.

Povey Cross to Hand Cross

Return along Povey Cross Road to the roundabout and take the last exit onto A23 London Road, traveling around the airport perimeter until the roundabout where the A23 turns south (Lowfield Heath). Continue on A23 through County Oak to roundabout with A2011. Take 2nd exit, London Road, into Crawley. Follow signs for A2219 through the town centre and out to the A23. Turn south and follow A23 to roundabout over M23. Take 2nd exit signposted Pease Pottage services. At roundabout past the Services take 3rd exit to Horsham Road, signposted Pease Pottage. Go as far as the Black Swan pub, then retrace route to roundabout and take 3rd exit south, B2114, Brighton Road, which becomes London Road. Continue to junction with B2110, turn right into Hand Cross.

*

After skirting the perimeter of the airport we pick up the old road at Lowfield Heath (*27 miles*). The road from here to Brighton was turnpiked in 1770, meaning that the entire route was then of good quality. The road ran through fields and past small hamlets to the roundabout at County Oak which was originally just one building standing on the Surrey/Sussex border.

Crawley (*30 miles*) was a very small country town at the time the coaches rolled though. At the entrance to the town was *The Rising Sun* inn and *The Half Moon* stood at the other end, allowing the coachman or guard to pose a riddle for the passengers: 'Why is Crawley the longest place in existence? Because the sun is at one end and the moon at the other.'

To see historic Crawley it is necessary to park and explore the pedestrianised High Street on foot. There are several old buildings to be seen including *The George*, now known lumpenly as the *Ramada Crawley Gatwick*. It was immortalized by Thomas Rowlandson in one of the illustrations for *An Excursion to*

Brighthelmstone by Henry Wigstead. Parts of the 16th century building remain, but it has had an eventful architectural life.

The George was, effectively, the halfway house between London and Brighton and the Prince Regent and Nelson are both known to have stayed there. It was also of major importance to enthusiasts of bare knuckle boxing, or pugilism, with bouts held at Copthorne and at Crawley Down attracting crowds of thousands.

The tiny hamlet of Pease Pottage, to the right of the road immediately after the M23 is crossed, was originally simply a toll gate (*31¼ miles*). If you go across the A23 you encounter the Old Brighton Road, but this is a dead end north and south. There appears to be no logical explanation for the name which is simply a variation on pease pudding, an old country dish. *The Black Swan* was an old inn close to the gate but the present building seems to be more modern.

The road begins to climb the Sussex Forest Ridge where originally forests of beech and hazel stretched for miles on either side. It is also a haunted stretch of road, according to ancient tales. 'Squire Powlett', a headless spectre, has the nasty habit of leaping onto the back of horses behind their riders and staying there until the edge of the forest was reached. The Hand Cross ghost seems to be less alarming and was given to playing practical jokes on the toll gate keepers.

The road has now reached a watershed with the rivers Mole and Medway flowing north and the Arun, Adur and Ouse flowing south.

Hand Cross, still a very small village, was originally just a tiny hamlet around a crossroads (*33½ miles*) and *The Red Lion*, now a gastro pub, was a prosperous coaching inn. The landlords also had a reputation for handling smuggled brandy of excellent quality.

The famous National Trust garden of Nymans is just south of Hand Cross. The house, now ruined, dates back to the 17th century but seems not to have had any importance on the early maps.

The Bolney and Hickstead route to Brighton branches off at Hand Cross. It was opened in 1813 and had a better surface, fewer steep hills and shaved about two miles off the distance.

Hand Cross to Brighton

Leave Hand Cross on the B2114 through Staplefield. Continue on Cuckfield Road down Hammer Hill and Holmsted Hill to Slough Green. Turn left on to B2115 Staplefield Road to Whitemans Green bearing right on to B2036 to Cuckfield. Keep on B2036 through the village to roundabout with A272. Take 2nd exit A272 to Ansty. Leave on the B2036 Cuckfield Road to roundabout with A273. Continue on B2036 through Burgess Hill to roundabout with A273. Continue on A273 to Pyecombe. Join the A23 through Patcham, Preston and down into the centre of Brighton at the Steine.

*

The road now descends the southern flank of the watershed across Staplefield Common (*34¾ miles*). This was famous for orchards of black cherries – 'black-hearts' – on which travellers would stop to feast. *The Dun Cow* inn was considered a good stopping place for both cherries and its famous rabbit pie.

The land begins to level out towards Slough Green (*36¼ miles*) and there used to be a lot of marshy hollows in the dips. The road swings left the hamlet of Whiteman's Green (*37¼ miles*) then curls south to the little town of Cuckfield (*37½ miles*). It was drawn by Rowlandson as a lively place with market stalls, a fashionable carriage passing through, a recruiting sergeant at work on gullible local lads and the spire of the parish church in the background.

From the 14th to the early 18th century this was where beds of iron ore were worked and the ironworks produced a wide range of products from firebacks to cannon. The railway missed Cuckfield and the nearest station was Haywards Heath to the east which grew from a tiny hamlet into a sizeable town while Cuckfield remains much as it always was.

The two main coaching inns were *The King's Head* on the corner of South Street and Church Street, now converted into residential units, and *The Talbot*, still on the High Street, but rebuilt.

Cuckfield Park, a 16th century house much altered in the mid-19th century, was the inspiration for Harrison Ainsworth's ghostly Gothic tale, *Rookwood*, published 1834.

Less than a mile further on is Ansty, once Handstay Cross, where the next turnpike gate was located.(*38 miles*) From Ansty the road crosses the River Adur (*40¼ miles*) and now runs through the densely built-up area of Haywards Heath. Until 1820 this was a wide stretch of heath, common land, scrub and fields with scattered farms and cottages. It was enclosed in the period up to

1855 and then vanished under houses and streets when the railway came through.

As the coach travellers arrived at *The King's Head* inn they would have probably been closely observed by the smugglers who apparently used the area to store contraband and would have averted their gaze from the occasional creaking gibbet where its hanged felon rotted as an awful warning.

Once out of Burgess Hill the road runs through farmland again, passing *The Friars Oak* inn (now rebuilt) on the left (*42¾ miles*). It was a well-known landmark for many years and even featured in one of Conan Doyle's stories, *Rodney Stone*.

Where the A273 crosses the B2116 was Stone Pound toll gate (*43½ miles*), the last but one of the nine gates between London and Brighton on this route. In 1836 there was such a heavy snowstorm across the country on Christmas Eve that the Mail coach leaving Brighton was stranded here after driving into a drift. Following his orders to get the mails through at all costs, the guard took one of the horses and abandoned the driver and three passengers. That was Sunday and he finally reached London at seven o'clock on Tuesday night. The driver and passengers managed to get back a mile to Clayton where they were snowed in for days.

Hassocks, to the east, is a town created from nothing by the arrival of the railways.

After Stone Pound the South Downs rise as a last barrier before the coast. The Downs are chalk with many dry valleys or deans and very few trees and in coaching days the crest had numerous windmills. This was sheep country with vast flocks gazing.

From the village of Clayton (*44½ miles*) the road climbs steeply to Pyecombe – or Piecombe as it is on the old maps (*45½ miles*). Pyecombe's Norman Church of the Transfiguration is situated on the pilgrimage route along the Downs from Winchester and Chichester to the tomb of Thomas à Becket at Canterbury. The next hamlet is Pangdean, almost lost under the widened A23. By the time the route crosses the A27 bypassing Brighton the remaining old villages have been swallowed up by the town.

Patcham (*48 miles*) was the location of a fatal encounter between one of the large smuggling gangs and soldiers and Excise officers in November 1796. On being challenged the gang fled, leaving their brandy behind, but Daniel Scales was shot in the head by a Riding Officer and was buried in Patcham churchyard on Church Hill. The church itself, although much 'restored' by the Victorians, retains a remarkable Last Judgement over the chancel arch. Close to the church is a fine 17th century circular dovecote with 550 nesting spaces. Pigeons were once a valuable food source.

From Patcham the road descended past the hamlets of Withdean and Preston (*49¾ miles*). The Georgian travellers would have still been in open country after Preston until they reached the junction with the road from Lewes where St Peter's church was built in 1824.

From here the visitor would be in Brighton and the road followed the line of gardens down to the Steine. The inns recommended in Cary's *New Itinerary... of the Great Roads* were *The Castle, The New Inn, The New Ship, The Old Ship, The St James's Tavern* and *The White Horse. (51½ miles).*

The Sutton and Reigate Variation of the 'Classic' Route

This route begins with the Westminster Bridge variation on the 'Classic' route and follows that route to Kennington.

Kennington to Mitcham

At the junction of the A23 and A3 in Kennington continue on the A3 to Clapham Common and take the A24 though Balam and Tooting Bec. At the junction by Tooting Broadway Underground station turn left onto A217, Mitcham Road.

*

With the Oval passed, and the Kennington tollgate negotiated, the 'Classic' route traffic parted company and headed for Streatham. The coaches on the route we now follow were travelling through old villages and hamlets linked together in a ribbon development that continued as far as Upper Tooting. But behind this string of houses were ancient farmlands and commons: London had not yet taken over.

The first hamlet encountered was Stockwell with *The Swan* inn, two miles from the Kennington tollgate. Stockwell soon ran into the bigger village of Clapham with its large triangular common that still maintains its old boundaries. (*4½ miles*). On the northern edge of the common stands Holy Trinity church, begun in 1774 to replace the medieval church that was in poor repair and considered unsuitable for the growing population of wealthy residents moving out of London to live around the Common. Cary's recommended inn, *The Plough,* was located on the site of the mock-Tudor building behind the Underground station.

Clapham would have been well known as the home of the Clapham Sect, a religiously devout group who fought for numerous humane causes but, most famously, for the abolition of slavery under the leadership of William Wilberforce. He lived in a house on the west side of the common.

The route ran down the eastern side of the common to the tiny hamlet of Balham Hill then on to Upper Tooting and Tooting, together comprising one very small linear village. In the middle of Tooting the road went to the east and then turned sharply south at a place known as Amen Corner and still called that today. (*6½ miles*)

The road ran south, passing an area of common land to the east called Figg's Marsh which is preserved today intact as a public park. After 1802 travellers would have been aware that they were passing very close to the home of Lord Nelson and Lady Hamilton at Merton Place, just to the west.

Mitcham (*8 miles*) lies on the River Wandle which runs north to the Thames. It was a large village with considerable industry based on the river and its mills and also on the various fragrant herbs grown in the area, especially lavender. The early maps show snuff mills, a calico drying ground and a brick yard. The extensive Mitcham Common, which has remained open, lies to the east of the road and the Surrey Iron Railway ran across it to form the link to the Wandle and its industries. [See the Classic route]

Mitcham to Reigate

Go through Mitcham on the A217 to the large oval roundabout with the A297. Little of historical interest is visible in Sutton and it is probably easier to bypass it by continuing on the A217. To follow the old route as closely as possible take the 2nd exit (Rose Hill) into Sutton. The road becomes Angel Hill, then High Street, Continue through the town's one-way system following signs for Reigate and rejoin the A217. Cross the M25 and continue on A217 up Reigate Hill.

*

Once through Mitcham the road leaves the straggling ribbons of housing behind and is in the open countryside to the next tollgate at Sutton, eleven miles from London and famous for mutton from the sheep grazed on the Downs immediately to the south.

The modern town retains so little of the past that it can well be bypassed on the A217. The roundabout at the northern end was the old crossroads of Stone Cot Hill, a mile from the start of the town. The main inn was *The Cock*, owned by the ex-pugilist 'Gentleman' Jackson. Its inn sign straddled the road as did that of *The Greyhound*. Both have been demolished.

The climb up Banstead Down must have been hard on the horses and the top of the Downs, once achieved, would have been an unpleasant place for travellers: open, windswept with only scattered cottages along the road. To the west lay Epsom racecourse, but otherwise there was just open pasture and tiny hamlets as the road descended towards Reigate and the valley of the Mole across Walton Heath.

Between Banstead and Burgh Heath is a short modern road called Tangier Wood. This is the approximate position of *The Tangier Inn*. It was originally the house of Admiral Matthew Buckle (1716-84) who named it after his corsair-hunting ground along the north coast of Africa. It then became an inn which was especially popular with post-chaise passengers. The story goes that George IV would always stop there for a glass of the landlady Miss Jeal's celebrated elderberry wine, served 'roking hot'.

There was a turnpike gate at Ruffet (*18 miles*), according to Cary – this is about where Lower Kingswood is today. The road continues on downwards until it reached the foot of Reigate Hill and *Gatton Inn* with Gatton Park to the left. (*19 miles*)

Reigate (*21 miles*) developed as a market town around an early medieval castle that was demolished in the 17th century. The historic part of the town is to the south of the castle around Bell Street and the High Street with a number of old buildings remaining. However, the main coaching inn, *The Swan*, with a gallows sign spanning the street, has long gone.

The road had to circle around the castle mound until, in 1823, the world's first road tunnel was dug underneath. It was pedestrianised in the 1970s and the traffic route is now back where it was before. Cobbett who visited Reigate when the tunnel was being built is scathing about how, '…in order to save a few hundred yards' length of road… the money of the country is actually thrown away.'

Built on soft sandstone, the town is riddled with passages and caves which are, in fact, sand mines. They are open only five days a year.

Reigate to Povey Cross

Leave Reigate on the A217 and follow it to the junction with Povey Cross Road.

*

Three miles out of Reigate was the tollgate at Wood Hatch at the crossroads where little Woodhatch Park is now. The road crosses the River Mole at what is now Sidlow Bridge, but was marked on the earlier maps as Kennersley Bridge. From there it was a long straight run through farmland and across Hookwood Common (*27½ miles*) to meet the 'Classic' route at Povey Cross.

The Old Route used from the 17th century

London to Blindley Heath

Follow the 'Classic' route as far as Purley then take the A22 to the roundabout junction with the M25. Take the 3rd exit B2255 to Godstone. At the roundabout take the 2nd exit onto A25 to Godstone Green. Where the road forks in the village take the left fork and continue to the B2236. Past the Bell Inn take the 2nd right, Tilburstow Hill. At the junction with the A22 turn right to Blindley Heath.

*

From the junction in Smitham Bottom the road ran over Riddles Down and crossed Kenley Common. At this point it picks up the Roman road running south from London. This doubtless took the easiest route over the high ground and would therefore have been the logical track to follow for slow, heavy vehicles over virtually unmade roads. The road bypassed the village of Caterham and then descended Godstone Hill to Godstone Green.

The original village was centred around the church of St Nicolas but shifted focus after the Black Death in 1342. From the 16th century Godstone Green became a major stopping place for wheeled traffic, with numerous inns and good watering ponds. Cary's *Itinerary* recommends *The White Hart* which still stands on the High Street.

Leaving the village the travellers would be faced with the long steep pull up Tilburstow Hill and then several miles of countryside relieved only by occasional farms and hamlets before reaching the turnpike gate just before Blindley Heath (*22 miles*). The heath itself was an area of common land surrounded by scattered cottages.

Blindley Heath to Forest Row

Continue on A22 to the roundabout with B2028 at Newchapel. Continue on A22 to junction with A262 at Felbridge. Continue on A22 into East Grinstead. Leave East Grinstead on A22. Fork left onto Hammerwood Road through Ashurst Wood, continue onto Wall Hill Road and rejoin A22 to Forest Row.

*

The road runs through open countryside and farmland and downhill to New Chapel (Newchapel) a small hamlet at a crossroads, now the location of a major Mormon temple.

From there it rises again through scattered woodland, the landscape still much as it would have been in the 1800s. The second turning on the left after the Newchapel roundabout, Wire Mill Lane, leads past a large hammer pond to *The Wiremill* pub. Originally this was a watermill for grinding wheat, powered by one of the tributaries of the River Eden, but in the 1560s the pond was created by damming the river and it became a hammer mill linked to a metal-working forge. In the early 1800s the map show it as Woodcock hammer mill, so presumably the metal working was still continuing.

The main road climbs steadily up Woodcock Hill and then descends to the crossroads hamlet of Felbridge on the county boundary *(26 ¾ miles.)* Now larger than it was in coaching days, it retains traces of Felbridge Park on the right before the crossroads.

The road into East Grinstead (*28 miles*) is now solidly built up, but the coach travellers would have passed a string of cottages and small houses scattered along the road before entering the town. In 1801 the town had 2,659 inhabitants and a flourishing general and cattle market. Cary's *Itinerary* recommends *The Dorset Arms* and *The Crown*. These two ancient pubs still stand in the High Street, part of one of the longest continual runs of 14th century timber-framed buildings in the country. The one-way system and restrictions mean that parking and walking is the best way to see them.

The Greenwich Meridian cuts through the High Street just to the east of St Swithun's church. The church itself was rebuilt in 1787 after lightening destroyed the medieval building. The architect was James Wyatt, designer of the Pantheon in Oxford Street and many fashionable country homes and Surveyor-General of the King's Works.

The coach traveller would have been out of the town at the point where the B2110 meets the High Street and the road begins a long climb through the tiny hamlet of Little Brockhurst to Ashurst Wood and Cherry Garden. Just over a mile from East Grinstead church the road reaches the top of the hill and Windmill Lane to the left marks where a mill once took advantage of the winds.

The left fork onto Hammerwood Road follows the original, steeper, route, dropping down into the hamlet of Ashurst Wood and then climbing again up Wall Hill Road to rejoin the A22 before dipping down again to the crossing of the little River Medway at Forest Row. (*31 Miles*)

Forest Row was a small village where the road to Tunbridge Wells forks off to the east. To the south and east of the village the royal hunting park of Ashdown Forest stretches away over the high ground. Originally established in the 13th century, and covering over twenty square miles, it is a 'forest' in the same sense as the New Forest – a hunting ground rather than a thickly wooded area.

To the west of the village are the moat and remains of Brambletye Castle. Cary's *Itinerary* advises, 'see on the r. the Ruins of Brambletide Castle.' In 1826 Horace Smith, the author of the hugely successful poetic parody *Rejected Addresses* (1812) and friend of Shelley, wrote a historical novel *Brambletye House*.

Forest Row to Uckfield

Continue on A22 through Wych Cross, Nutley to Maresfield. At roundabout with A272 take first exit (Batts Bridge Road) to Maresfield. Turn right into High Street, continue out of the village to roundabout with A26. Take 2nd exit, London Road, to Uckfield.

*

The two and a half miles from Forest Row to Wych Cross is a long, hard hill which must have been a strain on horses in either direction.

There was a toll gate at Wych Cross (*33 miles*) and here the road forks. The left hand fork, the modern A22, heads south-east, while the modern A275 goes directly south to Lewes. This right hand route would seem to be the more logical one for travellers heading for Brighton to take, but the turnpiked road took the other fork, perhaps because it was easier going, or perhaps because there were more villages along that route. Cary's *Itinerary* notes, 'On r. though Chailey to Lewes, 15 m[iles]' and that is only a mile shorter than the alternative.

The three miles to Nutley (*36 miles*) run through virtually unspoiled Ashdown Forest. It must have seemed wild and remote to the coach passengers who would probably have been glad to see *The White Hart* inn when they arrived in the village.

The turnpike trust responsible for the Eastbourne-London route, which the modern A22 follows closely, installed a series of milestones, cast in iron – probably locally from Wealden iron. They show the distance at the top, not from London but from a string of stylized bells representing Bow Bells. Many remain and the thirty six mile stone is in Nutley.

As well as iron working, smuggling was a thriving local industry in these parts and confrontations between smuggling gangs and the Excise officers were frequent and sometimes bloody.

The road continued for three miles to Maresfield, passing Cackle Street to the north-east. The road pattern has been changed considerably with the development for building of Maresfield Park, but the nearest approach to the original is by Batts Bridge Road from the A22. This takes you to the centre of the village with the church and, opposite it, *The Chequers* inn as recommended by Cary. At the junction with the High Street under the fingerpost to the left of *The Chequers* is another Bow Bells milestone. This shows forty one miles.

It is only two, very easy, miles to the town of Uckfield which probably meant that *The Maidenhead* inn received more traffic than *The Chequers* did. There is no sign of the inn today, but the High Street retains many Georgian houses and gives some feeling for how it must have looked as the coaches passed through.

Uckfield to Brighton

Continue along Uckfield High Street, fork right at the roundabout onto Lewes Road. Take 2nd exit at roundabout onto A26 towards Lewes. Take the A2029 into Lewes and High Street. Leaving Lewes on the Brighton Road A277 take the second exit from the roundabout (Ashcombe Hollow) and continue to the small car parking area where the road bends to the left to see the toll house. Return to the roundabout and take first exit onto A27 to Brighton through Falmer. Fork left onto A270 into Brighton to St Peter's Church.

*

Leaving Uckfield the Eastbourne turnpike forms the left fork at the roundabout. Our travellers would have continued on through Little Horstead (*43 miles*) to Lewes through well-watered farm land interspersed with numerous little woods and ponds.

Once past the hamlet of Ringmer the mass of Malling Down and the chalk face at Cliff looms up ahead to the east and the road skirts around it to the hamlet of Cliff where the tunnel for the A26 now cuts through. At this point travellers would have continued straight on for Newhaven Harbour or turned sharp right for Lewes High Street, crossing the River Ouse.

In 1801 Lewes had a population of 3,309 and was a flourishing port on the River Ouse where the river cuts through the South Downs. It is still the county town of East Sussex and in coaching days was the capital of the entire county.

The old part of the town lies on the west bank, with a steep climb from the bridge. When they reached the centre of town the coach traveller would have completed fifty miles from London and may well have refreshed themselves at *The Star* or *The White Hart*. *The White Hart* is still an impressive presence on the High Street. It was owned 1737 to 1760 by the chef William Verrall and extracts from his recipe book are still in print. He was trained in the Continental style of cookery and was determined to educate the English palate.

The hotel was often visited by Thomas Paine, revolutionary

and radical, author of *The Rights of Man* (1791). He formed the 'Headstrong Club' which met regularly here to debate issues.

The Star Inn was situated where the late 19th century Town Hall now stands on the High Street. Its cellars remain and are where a number of Protestant martyrs were held before being burned at the stake close by between 1555 and 1557.

Like many towns on or close to the South coast Lewes had a barracks, a sizeable encampment on the site of the present Lewes Prison. It also had a racecourse on the Downs lying due north of the modern roundabout where the Brighton Road out of Lewes meets the A27.

The traveller continuing on to Brighton would have encountered the next turnpike gate just beyond this roundabout. (*51¾ miles*) The A27 has obliterated most traces of the original features and junctions along this stretch but incredibly one of the original toll buildings remains. By taking the Ashcombe Hollow turning at the A27 roundabout it is possible to park right by what was the smaller of the two gate structures built in 1820. This one has a small grate and an oven while the larger building, designed to house the tollkeeper and his family, was on the other side of the road. That was demolished in 1868.

The rate of tolls levied by the Brighton-Lewes Turnpike Trust is painted on the side. 'For every horse, mare, gelding, mule, ass, bullock or beast of draft, drawing any waggon, cart or carriage of a like nature with wheels less breadth than six inches: 6d.' Vehicles with wider wheels, which were considered to cause less damage to the road surface were charged at 4½ d and a rider on a horse would pay 2d. Flocks and herds were also charged, by the score of animals.

Falmer (*54 miles*) is now much changed, with university campuses and the A27 dividing the village in half. The large village pond on the south of the road remains, somewhat diminished in size, and *The Swan* inn, mentioned by Cary, is still to be found to the north of the main road.

Just beyond Falmer is the entrance to Stanmer Park, the seat of the Earl of Chichester. The 18th century park, landscaped by Humphry Repton, is open to the public and the house (built 1772) is now a restaurant, wedding venue and tea room.

The A270 branches off from the A27 just after Falmer and follows the old road down into Brighton. This would have been open country in the early 19th century and travellers would have passed the manor house of Moulsecombe on the right, now extensively developed and part of the university campus. The area to the right of the road immediately south of Moulsecombe, now part of the campus and a business park, was the site of the Brighton barracks.

From there the road ran through open country passing the road to the racecourse on the left. The first races were here on Whitehawk Hill in 1784 and the Prince Regent was an enthusiastic supporter. A short distance further on the road meets the 'Classic' route at the junction where St Peter's church was built in 1824. At this point the traveller had arrived in Brighton.

The Bath Road

The first Pump Room for taking the waters was opened in Bath in 1706, a year after Beau Nash, the new spa's first Master of Ceremonies, arrived. Until then there was no pressing fashionable, or commercial, need to travel to Bath from London and there was no 'Bath Road' as such, just a road from London to the major port of Bristol and a tangle of lanes and tracks serving the villages and small towns between that and Bath. Antiquarians might visit to see the Roman remains, some travellers would join local people to try the mineral waters and marvel at the hot springs, but it was a difficult journey to undertake.

The Bristol road, which the route to Bath followed more or less to Marlborough, was not a fixed, well-surfaced, route until the turnpikes came. It meandered about with variations in the track between high and low ground depending on whether the road was flooded or what the weather was like. Even on such a relatively well-used road it was possible to get very lost amongst all these alternatives, as Samuel Pepys found in 1668 when he managed to lose his way between Newbury and Reading, two prosperous towns only seventeen miles apart.

The strip maps in John Ogilby's *Britannia* of 1675 show the London to Bristol road with three possible turnings to Bath indicated. These might look like modern roads on the map, but in reality they were deeply rutted and pot-holed, thick with mud and inadequately maintained by the reluctant inhabitants of each parish they passed through.

By the beginning of the 18th century turnpike roads, properly graded and surfaced and paid for by tolls, were beginning to appear. Each required an Act of Parliament, which was not cheap, but Bath began to turnpike the roads in its vicinity in 1706-7. Calne turnpiked three miles of road at the same time, claiming that the route was 'very ruinous and dangerous to all Her Majesty's subjects.' Turnpike Trusts were soon established and, section by section, the various 'Bath Roads' were improved, with the Act for the final section, Corsham to Bath via Box, passed in 1756.

This account traces the route as a stage coach traveller in 1800 might have experienced it, with detours along the way to alternative routes. By this date the work of the various Turnpike Trusts had levelled, graded and surfaced it to allow for safe, fast running and the Bath Road was considered to be the best road in England. It was well signed with fingerposts at crossroads and regular milestones and the taming of the heathlands and thickets, along with improved security measures, had greatly diminished the number of highwaymen.

It was also a very attractive route, so much so that *A Topographical Survey of the Great Road from London to Bath and Bristol with Historical and Descriptive Accounts of the Country, Towns, Villages, and Gentlemen's Seats on and Adjacent to It* was published in two volumes in 1792, illustrated by views of the scenery and landmarks.

The Stage Coaches

Despite the initial difficulties of the route, the earliest known stage coach service from London was advertised in 1657. It ran from the sign of *The Coach and Four Horses* in Queen Street every Monday and Thursday. In the same year the splendidly-named Onesiphorus Tapp of Marlborough advertised his service to "Redding, Nubery [Newbury], Marlborough, Bath or Bristol" from *The Red Lyon* in Fleet Street.

By 1667 there were several proprietors working the route including a 'Flying Machine' from *The Bell Savage* [*Belle Sauvage*] on Ludgate Hill. That took three days, 'God willing'. There would have been overnight stops along the way to rest the horses (although not necessarily the passengers) and the journey cost £1. 5 shillings – a significant amount of money.

By the early 1700s, as the practice of changing horses regularly was established, some coaches – 'Flyers' – were completing the journey in two days. They departed from London at 4 am while the more leisurely three day coaches would leave at 6am.

As the roads improved, the coaching business developed and the speed of the coaches increased. Prices fell, reliability improved and by the 1820s, even though Bath was no longer the highly fashionable draw it had once been, over twenty coaches left London for the city daily.

From the 1780s onwards coaches for Bath could be taken from *The Swan with Two Necks* in Lad Lane, Cheapside; *The Bolt-in-Tun*, Fleet Street; *The Saracen's Head* on Snow Hill and *The*

Golden Cross, situated where Nelson's Column now stands, to mention only some of the better known. Pierce Egan in his *Walks Through Bath* (1819) which is extensively quoted here, lists thirteen London inns despatching eighteen coaches between them to Bath.

Most of the coaches from the City also collected and put down at *The White Horse Cellar* in Piccadilly, located on the site where the *Ritz Hotel* now stands. It was so busy that it became a popular spot for sightseers.

As well as the stage and the Mail coaches – the invention of John Palmer, the Bath theatre owner, frustrated by the dreadful postal service – the Bath road would have carried post chaises, private coaches, heavy stage wagons, agricultural vehicles and riders, as well as flocks and herds of animals moving between the numerous market towns along the way.

In 1834 a count was made of the traffic through Maidenhead over a two week period: there were 2,230 horses drawing vehicles.

Following the Bath Road Today

This book guides the modern traveller along the route of the Bath Road in about 1800, with detours for the major alternatives. From Hyde Park Corner to Kensington it is considerably easier, and pleasanter, to travel by bus, hopping on and off. Beyond Kensington until Colnbrook it is, frankly, far better to follow the route on StreetView. Nothing can be seen of the old landmarks and the road is ugly, congested and not an enjoyable drive. The author has endured it so that you do not have to!

Picking up the route at Colnbrook ensures that you do not miss any of the remaining sights, although you do have to battle through Slough and it does not become a truly picturesque route until you pass Reading.

London to Kensington

Catch the number 9 bus from Green Park Underground station or, if travelling by car, take the A4 (Knightsbridge) from Hyde Park Corner, then A315 (Knightsbridge-Kensington Road-Kensington High Street).

*

Before boarding your Number 9 bus, take a moment to imagine the scene where *The Ritz* now stands at the north-east corner of Green Park. This was the site of *The White Horse Cellar* where the stage coaches from the City stopped to pick up the last London passengers and the incoming western coaches set down passengers including, on occasion, Jane Austen. It was a chaotic scene of milling vehicles, shoving passengers, porters, food sellers and gawking sightseers with pickpockets and touts adding to the perils.

Pierce Egan wrote in 1819, 'Whether the foot-step of the gay "set out" of the barouche or the more accommodating ladder to mount the roof of the *Regent* [coach], to the *coachy's* "All right – ya-hip!" and the sounding of the bugle by the guard to quit the bustle of the White Horse Cellar, the journey to most minds commences with pleasure and delight.'

Whether you swept past it in your private carriage, or you had taken your seat on the crowded stage, you drove past Green Park on the left and great mansions and hotels on the right, just as you do today, although most of the buildings you see now are later 19th century replacements.

Just before the end of Piccadilly, where the underpass plunges under Hyde Park Corner roundabout, is bus stop 'E' and next to it a high wooden shelf with cast iron supports. This is one of the few remaining porters' rests, where men could take the weight off their shoulders as they carried heavy loads around town.

On the other side of the road Old Park Lane emerges between the Hard Rock Café and the Rock Shop. This was where Park Lane used to join Piccadilly and there was a row of houses running from where the Hard Rock Café stands to what is now Apsley House, home of the Duke of Wellington, dominating Hyde Park Corner. Wellington's brother the Marquess Wellesley bought the house, developed it and sold it to his brother who remodelled it, while the other houses were gradually demolished leaving it standing in isolation as 'Number One London'.

The title does not come from the superiority of the house or its occupant but because we are now right on the western limit of London. In front stretches Knightsbridge and, when Jane Austen was staying with her brother Henry in his homes in Sloane Street and Hans Place, she was quite clear that Knightsbridge (or Knights Bridge, as it was known almost until the 19th century), was not London. 'If the Weather permits, Eliza & I walk into London this morng [sic].' she wrote in April 1809 from 64, Sloane Street.

Although the tentacles of development were reaching out from the new Sloane Street, down the Brompton Road and along towards Kensington, London still began at the Hyde Park Turnpike, situated until 1825 just about where Grosvenor Place meets Knightsbridge today. Mileages given in brackets are measured from this point.

Knights Bridge was never a parish or a manor, only a locality, known from Saxon times as Kyngesburig, or Knightsbrigg. There are many legends about the origins of the name, but none appear to have any basis in fact. The bridge in question crossed the Westbourne River as it left Hyde Park, where it had been dammed to form the Serpentine. The Westbourne ran on south along a meandering course which marks the boundary of Chelsea and St George's parishes to meet the Thames in the grounds of Chelsea Hospital. It was finally covered over in 1856/7 to become the unromantically-named Ranelagh Sewer and its outfall can still be seen at low tide. The Albert Gate of Hyde Park marks the point where it went under the road and William Street follows its line southwards.

If you had ventured this far in the time of the Tudors you would have encountered an appalling road, the 'Waye to Reading', mired so deep in mud that it contributed to the defeat of Sir Thomas Wyatt's rebel army. They marched against Queen Mary, but arrived so exhausted by the state of the 'road' that they were easy prey for the royal troops. Things did not greatly improve for hundreds of years and, even as late as 1842, reports speak of pavements ankle-deep in mud.

Worse than the mud were the highwaymen and footpads who infested this road. The last highway robbery on Knightsbridge was as late as 1799, after which a light horse patrol was sent out from the barracks to patrol the road and it was one of the earliest to have street lighting. Mr Davis in his *History of Knightsbridge* (1854) records that even after the armed patrols were instituted, 'pedestrians walked to and from Kensington in bands sufficient to ensure mutual protection, starting their journey only at known intervals, of which a bell gave due warning.'

Just before leaving London through the Hyde Park Corner tollgate was St George's Hospital, at the junction with Grosvenor Place. It is still there, but is now the *Lanesborough Hotel*. It was originally opened in Lanesborough House in 1733, but was rebuilt in 1827. Behind it was Tattersall's sale ring, the meeting place of choice for the Georgian and Victorian gentleman and sportsman until 1865.

The northern edge of the road bounding Hyde Park was lined by a high brick wall except where houses or inns had been built, so, unless they were seated on top of a coach, travellers would not have had a view into the Park as they passed.

Going east we would have encountered *The White Hart* inn on the north side and a barracks for foot soldiers (demolished 1836) on the south. The narrow entrance to Old Barrack Yard still marks the spot. We cross the Westbourne as we pass William Street, where today there is the unlovely round tower of the *Sheraton Hotel*. Once this was the site of a house owned by a Mr Lowndes. Behind it, where Lowndes Square is now, was a rural pleasure garden, Spring Garden (not to be confused with the one of the same name at Admiralty Arch) at the sign of *The World's End*. It is referred to in Pepys's diaries several times, including in the final entry, May 31st 1669: 'To the Park, Mary Botelier and a Dutch gentleman, a friend of hers being with us. Thence to the "World's End" a drinking house by the Park, and there merry, and so home late.'

More or less opposite was Trinity Chapel which was probably medieval in origin and functioned as a hospital, or lazar house, for the poor. Traditionally it was said to have taken in plague victims in 1665 and the dead were buried opposite, under Knightsbridge Green at the present junction of Knightsbridge, Sloane Street and Brompton Road. Eventually the chapel fell into total disrepair and was rebuilt. Its present incarnation is further along the road in Kensington.

For many years, until the passing of Lord Hardwicke's Marriage Act in 1753, it was the location for irregular, clandestine or runaway marriages and the registers for the chapel contain entries with notes such as 'secrecy for life' or 'secret for fourteen years' added to them. Possibly the most famous person married there was Prime Minister Sir Robert Walpole who wed a daughter of the Lord Mayor of London.

Directly opposite the site of Spring Garden the Albert Gate (built 1846) opens into Hyde Park and here the Westbourne passes under the road. On the park side of the bridge was *The Fox and Bull* inn, patronised by artists such as George Morland and Sir Joshua Reynolds, who painted its sign. Less pleasantly, it was a receiving house for the Humane Society, founded to assist drowning persons or to deal with their bodies. It was to this inn that the body of Harriet Shelley, the poet's first wife, was brought after she drowned herself in the Serpentine in 1816.

Immediately after *The Fox and Bull* was the Cannon Brewery, so called from the cannon mounted on its roof. That was surrounded by 'low and filthy courts with open cellars' – a far cry from the elegant Kuwaiti and French Embassy buildings which occupy the site now. Behind the bulk of the embassies the gate pillars are topped by two bronze stags that were originally on the Ranger's Lodge of Green Park.

Just past the brewery were the barracks for the Horse Guards, giving them direct access into Hyde Park, just as they have today. Originally built in 1794/5, the barracks were rebuilt in 1878/9 and then again in the 20th century, slightly further west on Knightsbridge. From here onwards there were virtually no buildings on the north side, only the brick wall of the park.

Just past this point is the junction with Sloane Street, developed after 1780 along an old track from the King's Road in Chelsea. Another old road, the Brompton Road, comes in at an angle at the same point and led to the village of Brompton and on to Fulham. At the junction was Knightsbridge Green with a watch house for the constable, a pound for straying livestock, and possibly the site of Trinity Chapel's plague pit. This was the point where the granite sets that made up the road surface ceased and the mud really began. It is also close to here that Tattersall's moved in 1865.

On the south side of Knightsbridge, after the Brompton Road turning, were *The Rose and Crown*, the oldest of Knightsbridge's inns, and *The Old King's Head* and then the floor-cloth manufactory of Messrs. Smith and Barber. It had been established in 1754 and lasted well into the Victorian era.

Then came three mansions that were, when they were built, true 'country houses'. The first was Rutland House, the next Kent House, home for a while to the Duke of Kent, Queen Victoria's father, and then Kingston House. Kingston House was built in 1769 for the scandalous Elizabeth Chudleigh. She died in 1796 and it later became the home of the Marquess Wellesley who died there in 1842.

An area of nursery gardens followed on the south side of the road, part of the great expanse of fruit and vegetable-producing land that surrounded London. Somewhere along this stretch we enter what is now known as Kensington Gore – nothing to do with blood, but named after Gore House.

Before we reach the Royal Albert Hall we pass the Prince of Wales's Gate entrance to Hyde Park (now opposite Ennismore Gardens). Exactly where the gate is was *The Halfway House* inn, a most insalubrious neighbour for a fine mansion. This was where the 'carriers' or 'cruisers', spies for the highwaymen of Hounslow Heath, would congregate to see who was travelling and pass the word on to alert the highwaymen about fine carriages or vulnerable riders.

In April 1740 the Bristol postboy was held up here by a footpad and in 1774 three highwaymen were hanged on this spot, presumably intended as a strong hint to the habitués of the inn. Just beyond the inn was the first milestone from the Hyde Park turnpike.

Gore House stood on the site of the Royal Albert Hall. It was built in the 1750s, decorated by Robert Adam and was the home in the 1780s of Admiral Lord Rodney. It was acquired in 1808 by William Wilberforce, the great campaigner for the abolition of the slave trade, who lived there until 1821. Its final use before it was demolished was as a restaurant to serve the visitors to the Great Exhibition of 1851, under the supervision of celebrity chef Alexis Soyer.

John Wilkes, a London alderman and the Member of Parliament for Aylesbury, lived on Kensington Gore. He owned the radical newspaper *The North Briton* and in 1763 was arrested and sent to the Tower for libelling the King. The offending newspaper was burned by the public hangman, but Parliament declared the warrant to be illegal. In 1774 Wilkes became Lord Mayor of London.

Just after the Albert Hall the road begins to curve northwards to the western end of the park and the beginning of the village of Kensington, the point where we can leave the dangers of Knightsbridge behind us with a sigh of relief for our arrival safe from the mud and the footpads.

At the start of the curve is Queen's Gate, or Hogmire Lane as it was when the first turnpike after London was reached at this point. Immediately after it, on the park side of the road, stood the barracks for the troops guarding Kensington Palace. Opposite the barracks was the high brick wall of Kensington House, once the home of Louise de Kérouaille, one of Charles II's mistresses.

The traveller would now pass a number of inns and ale houses on both sides of the road. *The Goat and Compasses*, *The Three Tuns*, *The Marquess of Granby* and *The King and Queen* were side by side between Hogmire Lane and Love Lane (now Victoria Road) on the southern side up to Young Street. Opposite were *The King's Arms* – at the point where the road was paved with granite setts again – *The Duke of Cumberland*, *The Bunch of Grapes* and *The Civet Cat*, between the barracks and Church Lane, now Kensington Church Street.

On the western corner of Church Lane stands the church of St Mary Abbot (*1¾ miles*). There has been a church on the site since at least 1262. The medieval church was replaced in the late 17th century, when the relocation of the Court to Kensington Palace greatly increased the congregation, and that was the church the Georgian traveller would have seen. Charles G. Harper, writing in 1899, remembered it from his childhood and described it as 'a hideous structure.' It was demolished as being too small and rebuilt in 1872. Many of the monuments from the old church were moved into it and it also retains the two charity school figures of a boy and girl in blue uniforms on a building in the churchyard on the northern side.

Kensington was an exceedingly busy village, especially in the evening when the eight o'clock Mails went through, competing with all the other traffic to get into London before darkness fell. A watch house stood on the corner of the High Street and Church

Lane and the parish stocks stood in the churchyard. More inns lined the High Street, ending with *The Star and Garter* where the next toll gate spanned the road at the junction with Earl's Court Lane (now Earls' Court Road) to the south and the eastern edge of Holland House's grounds.

To the north, immediately after the toll gate, stands Holland House in the remains of its grounds. It was originally built in 1605 in a park of over five hundred acres which shrank over the years as land was sold off. In 1721 it was bought by the Edwardes family and leased from 1746 by Henry Fox, 1st Baron Holland, who bought it outright in 1767. Under his son Henry, the third Baron (1773-1840), an active politician, the house became a major literary, artistic and political meeting place. Visitors included Byron, Thomas Macaulay, Benjamin Disraeli, Charles Dickens and Sir Walter Scott and passing travellers would have craned to get a glimpse of such a well-known house.

Until the beginning of the 19th century the road from this point ran through open farmland, nursery gardens and countryside, but London was expanding and from 1811 the elegant Earl's Terrace was built on the southern side of the road immediately after the toll gate, with the charming Edwardes' Square behind it. Both retain their houses intact.

Kensington to Hounslow

The Number 9 bus continues as far as Hounslow. Drivers should continue on the A315.

*

After the Holland Park toll gate the next landmark was the

Counters Brook, running under the road on its way to Stamford Bridge and its outlet at the Thames, now known as Chelsea Creek. Its original course is difficult to pin down, but it appears to have run more or less where the railway and Underground lines go under the road, just before Olympia.

Hammersmith turnpike (*3¼ miles*) spanned the road just before Brook Green Road, which still runs off to the right, although Victorian and more modern development has obliterated most of the old lanes the coach travellers would have seen. *The Bell and Anchor* inn, on the right just after the turnpike, was one of the possible first changes for carriages leaving London.

On the corner of the next road on the left (Colet Gardens) stands a pub called *Latymers,* built in the early 1900s on the site of *The Red Cow.* This was a 16th century inn much favoured by footpads who passed on intelligence to highwaymen. It was particularly favourable for the purpose, because this was another major staging point from London where many coaches would stop for a change of horses. It had a large range of stables and was also a stopping place for the wagoners who took fruit and vegetables in to Covent Garden and hay and straw for London's thousands of horses.

The modern road improvements and relentless development of this area have left nothing for the modern visitor to see, unfortunately, but the coach traveller would have viewed a number of schools and academies as well as private houses, shops and inns. There was even a rumour that certain of the royals kept their mistresses in Hammersmith which was considered to be a desirable and healthy place to live.

The river is only a short distance from the road once we enter King Street and there was a small dock for market garden produce, supplies for the vast Cromwell brewery and for pleasure boats.

Continuing west along King Street we pass a small patch of green space to the north. This opens up into the much larger Ravenscourt Park. The 1800 travellers would have known it as Paddenswyck, or Paddingwick, Park which had once contained an ancient moated house with, behind it, Starch Green where the local people bred rabbits for the London meat trade. It was also where the gibbets stood to display hanged criminals.

Next to the park was the hamlet of Goggle Goose Green whose name does not appear to be preserved in any modern streets. As our road becomes Chiswick High Road the stagecoaches would now be entering Turnham Green but, although the name is still to be found, Chiswick has expanded north from the river to swallow up the little hamlet.

Turnham Green was the site of a Civil War skirmish in 1642 when the Royalists held back the Parliamentary forces to enable the King and his court to make a safe retreat to Oxford. It was also the home of the notorious poisoner, Thomas Griffiths Wainewright (1794 -1847) whose career inspired stories by Conan Doyle and Dickens. The location of his home is now under Linden Gardens – ironically very close to the modern police station.

A tiny remnant of Turnham Green's common survives in the angle of the High Road and Heathfield Terrace and *The Old Pack*

Horse inn, which was rebuilt in 1910, stands on the corner of the High Road and Acton Lane (B409). In 1696 it was the headquarters of a plot to assassinate King William III and restore James II to the throne. The scheme was betrayed and the conspirators hanged, drawn and quartered. It was also the haunt of highwayman Jack 'Sixteen-string' Rann who had his last drink there before attempting to rob Princess Amelia's chaplain. He was hanged for his trouble in 1774. The name came from the number of strings, or laces, at the knees of his breeches, a fashionable extravagance in the mid-18th century.

Jack was not the only highwayman in the area and robberies were almost too commonplace to report. However, this did not deter the writer and dilettante Horace Walpole who always stopped here for refreshments when travelling between his house Strawberry Hill and London. In 1717 the travellers in *A Journey to Bath and Bristol* took their breakfast of amber ale and spice cake at Turnham Green and it seems to have remained a popular refreshment stop into the Regency periods.

The Four Horse Club, founded in 1808, consisted of gentlemen enthusiasts who drove private coaches known as 'park drags', very similar in design to Mail coaches, with teams of four blood horses. They would meet on the first and third Thursdays in May and June and drive from Cavendish Square to Salt Hill. Their regular luncheon for thirty members was ready for them at *The Pack Horse* where they drank cider cup before continuing on to Hounslow Heath.

The six mile stone would have stood somewhere beneath the

modern Chiswick roundabout where the M4 crosses the North and South Circular Roads and the Chiswick High Road turns south towards Kew Bridge. The present bridge was built in 1903 but we do not cross it, instead turning westward into Brentford, the county town of the old county of Middlesex. It does not seem to have been a particularly imposing or attractive place in the past, although its history includes a visit by Julius Caesar who forded the Thames here in 54BC, and battles in 1016 and 1642. The 1717 *A Journey to Bath and Bristol* describes it as, 'A famous place for Dirt.'

Pierce Egan wrote, 'The traveller is at length awakened... by the long, stony, jolting town of Brentford, consisting of upwards of 300 houses, irregularly built, and containing nearly 2,000 inhabitants...On the left of Brentford is seen Kew-Bridge; and at various parts of the town the new palace [Kew Palace], built under the immediate direction of HIS MAJESTY...is viewed across the river with a pleasing effect, and generally considered an ornament to Brentford.'

Brentford is located where the River Brent – a mere eighteen miles long – joins the Thames. Where the Bath Road crosses it has been canalised as part of the Grand Junction Canal.

Syon Park, the 'capacious and elegant mansion' (Egan) of the Duke of Northumberland lies to the south of the road as it leaves Brentford, and Osterley Park, the summer home of the Earl of Jersey, lies to the north west. The Countess of Jersey was one of the Patronesses of Almack's and thus a key figure in the late Georgian social scene. The house was left to her by her grandfather, Robert Child the banker, who wanted to cut out her mother who had eloped with the Earl of Westmorland against Child's wishes. According to Egan, 'This circumstance, which once so agitated the fashionable world, is now got rid of in the mind of the traveller by his arrival at Smallberry-Green.' Eight miles from London this tiny hamlet was the residence of Sir Joseph Banks (1743-1820) the botanist, naturalist and one of the leading scientists of his day.

'Sir Joseph, fav'rite of great queens and kings,

Whose wisdom weed and insect hunter sings...' (Paul Pindar)

In coaching days the long and straggling village of Hounslow lay between the nine and ten mile stones. Its High Street is now one-way, which makes it difficult to drive along the old route, but nothing remains of the old coaching village to make walking through really worthwhile. Pierce Egan was of the same opinion. 'Hounslow, a town of little note; and, although time is afforded the traveller to exercise his mind while the horses are changing, and "*coachy*" is taking his little *whet*, yet no objects present themselves worthy of his immediate attention.'

Hounslow was of major importance before the railways came because the Exeter and Land's End road branched off the Bristol and Bath road here, as did the road to Windsor. Two thousand post horses were stabled in the town and the movement of coaches and chaises was non-stop. *The George*, on the southern side of the High Street, was the main inn. It has been estimated that one hundred and seventy coaches went through daily. All this

171

went with the arrival of the railways and the depressing effects on the local economy were obvious even as early as 1842.

Hounslow to Slough

Leave Hounslow on the A3006 to join the A4 (Bath Road). Follow the A4 along the northern edge of Heathrow Airport. Turn left onto the A3044 (Stanwell Moor Road) then take the third exit at first roundabout onto Bath Road. Go through Colnbrook to rejoin the A4 westwards. Go under the M4 continuing into Slough on the A4.

*

The Bath Road strikes out north-west from Hounslow, crossing an area that was once the notorious 4,293 acres (6.71 square miles) of Hounslow Heath. Today a nature reserve of 200 acres is all that remains of the flat, scrubby, area pockmarked by gravel pits and with only scattered hamlets. In the 18th and 19th century it was good for nothing but gravel extraction, grazing inferior sheep and for siting gunpowder factories which could blow up regularly without too much damage to anything around them. Heathrow Airport has covered most of the heathland but the route of the Bath Road still follows its old track, preserved along the northern edge of the airport.

The Heath was notorious during the 17th and 18th centuries for its highwaymen, who found rich pickings from both the Bath and the Exeter roads, to say nothing of all the traffic to the court at Windsor.

Probably the most famous highwayman of the Heath, or perhaps the one with the most romantic legend, was Claude du

Vall who was executed in 1670. He was reputed to have robbed with great courtesy and even allowed one couple to go unmolested after the lady had agreed to dance with him.

The road was liberally decorated with a succession of gibbets where offenders' bodies hung rotting as an example to others. They appear to have been removed from about 1800, which must have made the scene more pleasant for travellers.

By 1817 Pierce Egan contended that, 'Hounslow-Heath has become almost as safe as riding through St James's Park [with] …all the palpitations of the heart, shiverings and cold sweats, which formerly operated upon the delicate feelings of the female passengers, under the apprehension of being robbed every instant…now completely removed.' The 19th century traveller was not entirely secure however – a Mr Steele was murdered in 1802, for example. The men responsible, Haggarty and Holloway, were hanged – and twenty eight of the onlookers at the Old Bailey execution were killed in the crush. The robbers of the Bristol Mail in 1820 were more fortunate and got clear away.

The road turns west at Cranford Bridge where it crossed the little River Crane, now virtually invisible. This was the location of *The Berkeley Arms* and *The White Hart,* with Cranford Park, seat of the Earls of Berkeley, to the north of them. As late as 1890 Charles G. Harper could describe Cranford village as, 'rich in beautiful old mansions set in midst of walled gardens.' Now they are lost under modern housing, trading depots and the M4.

From Cranford Bridge the road led through Harlington Corner (now the junction with the A437) where the slow local coaches set down passengers for Uxbridge at *The Magpies*. This inn was the second refreshment stop for the Four Horse Club where they downed more cider cup made with hock and borage.

A kilometre further on (0.62 miles) the first left turn leads into Nene Road, part of the Northern Perimeter roads of the airport. This is the location of King's Arbour, a barn which, according to local legend, was used as stabling by King George III. More certainly it was the end of the Ordnance Survey's baseline set out by Major General William Roy in the summer of 1784. This formed the basis for the entire survey of the British Isles to produce the famous Ordnance Survey maps. The other end of the 27,404.01 (5.1 miles) line was the Hampton Poor House to the south. The ends of the line are marked by upturned cannon barrels and the King's Arbour one can be seen by the side of Nene Road.

Continuing along the A4, the line of the Bath Road goes off to the left to Longford, just past the right-hand turning to the A3044. It is possible to drive down it far enough to see, on the left, one of the pumps that were installed to keep down the dust. A little further on it is 'No Entry' for cars, so it is necessary return to the A4 and to drive on to the left turn onto the A3044 (Stanwell Moor Road). At the first roundabout it is possible to turn back into Longford, although there is nothing ancient to be seen now. A Tudor waterway, The Duke of Northumberland's River, runs through it.

The River Colne is multi-branched between Longford and Colnbrook and the area is low-lying and marshy. Returning to the roundabout and taking the last exit (Bath Road) towards

Colnbrook, one crosses the King's Bridge (now under the roundabout), then the Moor Bridge and the Mad Bridge. The road becomes The Old Bath Road, then Park Street as you enter Colnbrook.

Colnbrook, sixteen miles from London, is almost a shock after the traffic and the modern sprawl all the way to Longford. It still looks much as it must have done to coach passengers with cottages, old houses and brick walls and a series of substantial inns – *The Star and Garter* on the left as you drive up Park Street, *The George* as you enter the High Street, and the Elizabethan *Ostrich*. *The George*, according to Ned Ward's 1700 story *A Step to Bath*, was 'an Inn famous for Extravagant Bills and Short Commons.'

However, it had a better reputation than *The Ostrich*. According to local legend it had belonged in the 14th century to a Sweeny Todd-like landlord who dropped his victims from their beds, through a trap door, into the brew house vat beneath. He is supposed to have accounted for sixty one victims before he was found out and hanged. Stagecoach drivers relied on gruesome stories such as these to enliven the journey for the rooftop passengers and hence to increase the size of their tip.

The River Colne is crossed by a bridge of 1777, just where Park Street becomes Bridge Street before meeting High Street, and the little brook forms the boundary between the counties of Middlesex and Buckinghamshire.

It is a nasty jolt back to modernity to leave Colnbrook, rejoin the A4 and find oneself in the outskirts of Slough. On the Old Series Ordnance Survey map, which shows the road as our coach passengers would have seen it, Slough is a village barely half a mile in length, located at the junction of the Bath Road with the road from Eton and Windsor (now the A332). Now the town extends along seven miles from the point where we rejoin the A4 to its western edge where only a few fields separate it from Maidenhead.

Slough to Reading

A4 to Hare Hatch. Fork left onto A3032 through Twyford. Rejoin A4 to Reading.

*

When travelling between Windsor Castle and St James's Palace the royal family and the Court would pass through Datchett to join the Bath Road at about the point where Junction 5 of the M4 is now.

The hamlets and farms surrounding Slough – Langley Marsh, Langley Broom, Upton – have been swallowed by the town.

Driving past the town centre between the A412 and B416 roundabouts the Observatory shopping mall is prominent on the left. This commemorates Slough's greatest resident, the astronomer Sir William Herschel (1738-1822). He lived at Observatory House, just behind where the mall is now, from 1786 until his death with Caroline, his sister and fellow leading astronomer. As King's Astronomer he was frequently at Windsor and he constructed a massive 40 inch telescope in the garden. The house survived until 1963 when it was demolished. Herschel was a celebrity in his lifetime and would have been of great interest to travellers along the Bath Road. Certainly Pierce Egan considered that Slough was made 'rather attractive' by the connection.

In July 1787 Colonel John Byng stayed at *The Crown* and wrote, 'Having order'd supper we express'd our wishes to see Dr Herschel's astronomical glasses; which our landlord said would be permitted us on sending a note to the doctor, who gave us leave to walk into the garden and see the outside of his instruments – and nothing else!' One can hardly blame Doctor Herschel for not satisfying the curiosity of every passing gentleman! However, Byng recovered his temper later after making punch for himself and his companions, 'which made us laugh at our being taken in by our foolish hopes of being able to see the new discoveries in the moon.'

The 1748 edition of Daniel Defoe's *Tour* remarked that Slough seemed to consist of little other than inns: 'They seem to vie with one another, and 'tis wonderful how they all subsist; especially as they are opposed by the two famous new ones of The Castle and Windmill, a little way out of Slough, which are much more delightfully situated, and have better Accommodations.'

Colonel Byng frequently passed through Slough on his travels. He stayed twice in July 1785 with his companion Colonel Bertie and put up at *The Crown*, 'a good inn.' 'We took a lounging walk before supper,' he reported on the first occasion, 'and then attacked the roast fowl, for which this inn is famous.'

He slept badly. 'What with a hot night, and my legs slipping every minute through my own torn sheet, I did not sleep as comfortably as I expected.'

Returning later that month, he wrote '...in no house have we met with better fare or better beds.' Despite that, his earlier remark about his own sheets reminds us that travellers often packed their own bedding to be certain that it was aired and, hopefully, kept the bugs at bay.

Once through the village of Slough the road ran down Salt Hill into the valley of a little stream making its way south to the Thames. The views of Windsor Castle and Eton College from the top of the hill here were considered very fine.

The little hamlet of Salt Hill was a major staging point for coaches and *The Castle* and *The Windmill* inns that Defoe described grew prosperous until the arrival of the railway in 1838 killed their trade. The members of the Four Horse Club dined alternately at the two inns – apparently exceedingly well – and then drove back to London the next morning.

The only relic of the Slough area that the traveller of 1800 would recognise is the Montem Mound, an ancient tumulus. It was the destination for the Eton College Montem, an annual procession of the boys in fancy costumes, accompanied by bands and a vast crowd of onlookers, from Eton College. They solicited alms, or 'salt', as they went, hence the name of Salt Hill. The last Montem was held in 1844.

The Montem Mound itself can just be glimpsed after crossing the railway and travelling down the hill with Salt Hill Park to the right. There is a set of traffic lights and a road to the left and the mound sits in the middle of a tiny patch of open ground, much eroded and diminished.

After these traffic lights the road continues, now through the vast Slough Trading Estate, but once across open farmland. A long, shallow, curve to the left marks the point where Ash Mill stood on Two Mile Brook. Before the Thames was reliably bridged at Maidenhead the route went off north-west here, through Burnham, Cliveden woods, across the Thames by ferry to Cookham and south again to rejoin the road at Maidenhead thicket.

Maidenhead's first bridge was built in 1297 but it cannot have been very safe, as traffic continued to take the wide detour until 1771 when the current bridge was constructed. It replaced a succession of timber versions which were 'maintained' in the Middle Ages by hermits licenced to beg there by the Bishop of Salisbury.

Today, following the later 18th century route towards Maidenhead, we travel on and, after passing through the neighbourhoods of Cippenham and Burnham – once hamlets – the built-up area begins to be broken up by fields as the road descends towards the Thames. Under the railway bridge, at the crossroads with Berry Hill leading north to Taplow village, stood *The Dumb Bell* inn.

Once across the 'light and elegant' Maidenhead bridge (Egan) travellers would have had to pay a toll and would then arrive at *The Orkney Arms*, otherwise known as *Skindle's* after its landlord. In 1792 Archibald Robertson wrote, 'At the end of Maidenhead Bridge stands an excellent inn, where travellers are well accommodated and parties often resort together for the amusement of fishing.'

The High Street (*26 miles*), which would have been the main road through the town, is now partially pedestrianised, so it is tricky to drive down and probably best explored on foot. All the main inns were located here and *The Red Lion, The Saracen's Head, The Sun, The White Hart* and *The Bear* were the chief establishments.

The Bear was the main inn and did a good trade with travellers who preferred to sleep there and cross the notorious Maidenhead Thicket in broad daylight. Its size and importance is shown by the fact that thirty five coach horses were killed when its stables burned down in 1835. Only one horse was saved, named Miraculous, and it continued to work on the Bristol Mail for years afterwards. *The Bear* was rebuilt in 1845 and has a fine porch topped with a large black bear.

The centre of the High Street was narrowed by the chapel of St Andrew which stood in the middle of the road and was not removed until 1824. Given that over ninety coaches a day passed through the town, this must have been a considerable bottleneck.

Once through Maidenhead travellers had to negotiate the Thicket. Coaches for Henley left before it, turning right on what is now Henley Road just before the Bath Road crosses the A404(M), but the Bath Road continued through the wooded area with its lurking footpads and highwaymen.

In 1717 the travellers on *A Journey to Bath and Bristol* reported:

'We now came to the famous Woods of old,

Where Trav'llers often lose their darling Gold,

Where cunning Thief with a tremendous Hand,

From thicket Rushes, bids the Coachman Stand.'

Once safely through Maidenhead Thicket coaches reached Littlewick Green and the modern traveller is in the countryside for the first time since leaving London.

The road goes down Knowl Hill, through Kiln Green and into Hare Hatch where the way was lined with small chalk quarries. Then the land dips once more into the valley of the Thames. The road went into Twyford (*33 miles*), where a change of horses would be made at *The King's Arms* inn, and then crossed the little River Lodden.

There is a hill to climb out of the valley with a view for the passengers on top of the stagecoach of the valley of the Thames to their right and Reading ahead of them.

Reading to Speen

Enter Reading on the A4 (London Road, then Crown Street). Turn right onto the A327 (Southampton Street). Cross the roundabout (2nd exit Bridge Street), cross the River Kennet, 2nd left into Castle Street, across roundabout onto A4155 (Castle Hill, then Bath Road) which becomes the A4. Follow the A4 to the M4. Take the first right after the motorway into Theale, then left into High Street. Rejoin the A4 at the far end and continue to Newbury. At the roundabout with the A339 take 2nd exit (London Road). At next roundabout 2nd exit (Oxford Street). At next roundabout 1st exit (Old Bath Road) to the A4. Turn left.

*

In Reading (*38 miles*) the Bath Road takes a sharp right-left to cross the River Kennet. Reading was the location of one of the greatest abbeys in pre-Reformation England and it remained a prosperous market town. Egan describes it as, 'a corporate town of considerable interest and extent. It contains numerous excellent buildings, some good streets, several churches and a theatre. The inhabitants are calculated at about 11,000, and the number of houses between 2 and 3,000. A great deal of business is carried on in Reading.'

Later in the century Victorian industry in the shape of Huntley and Palmer's biscuit factory caused a rapid expansion. The main inns for coaches were *The Bear* and *The Crown*. Colonel Byng was not impressed with *The Black Bear* on a visit in July 1787. 'Supper order'd, and quickly served. With a bowl (again) of sour and weak punch…when I went to bed I fancied the sheets damp and so to my sides there were only blankets.' In 1833 Isambard Kingdom Brunel stayed at the same inn in the course of surveying the route of the Great Western's London to Bristol line.

The climb out of Reading is fairly steep, but it takes the road along the flanks of the hills overlooking the valley of the Kennet, high enough to be safe from flooding. From there to Newbury it remains reasonably level, which allowed carriages to get up some speed, although at the cost of a great deal of dust in dry weather.

All along the Bath Road from Cranford Bridge on Hounslow Heath, pumps were set up to water the road to keep the dust down. A handful of these remain, a reminder that even well-made turnpike roads did not have a tarred surface. One example, quite difficult to spot because it is so dark and rusty, is on the left hand side of the road in Calcot.

Mud rather than dust appears to have been the problem in the 17th century. Celia Fiennes in her *Journeys* (c.1690) recorded, 'from Redding to Theale sad clay deep way; thence to Newbury all clay mirey ground.'

Before reaching Calcot Row, which was only a few cottages in those days, the traveller would pass on the right hand side Prospect Park and then Calcot Park. These would have been a great interest as the location for the *Ballad of the Berkshire Lady* and the romantic tale of the heiress Miss Frances Kendrick of Calcot Park who, in 1707, masked, challenged the man she loved to duel with her or marry her. The gentleman, a lawyer, decided to take a chance on who was behind the mask and agreed to the wedding and it proved to be a true love match. After her death he built himself Prospect House with a view of the woods where she challenged him.

Theale, the next little village, is forty three miles from the Hyde Park turnpike and was the point where the stagecoach drivers, who would have driven about fifty miles from the City, would hand over their vehicle at *The Falcon* inn and take a rest before driving a coach back. Drivers would expect the passengers to tip them before they drove on, a process known as 'kicking the passengers' who would recognise the polite, 'Gentlemen, I am leaving you now,' and a touch of the hat brim as their cue to pay up. The guard would do the whole journey, however long.

Ned Ward, in 1700, partook of 'Bottle Ale and Plumb-Cakes' at *The Bell*. Both *The Falcon* and *The Bull* are still recognisably old coaching inns and the width of the attractive village street hints at how busy it used to be.

Deadman's Lane, a turning to the right off the High Street, marks the spot where Prince Rupert's Royalist forces attacked the Parliamentarian Earl of Essex in the course of the first Battle of Newbury (1643). The attack was so savage that it swung the narrowly-fought battle in the Royalist favour.

From Theale the road comes down into the valley of the Kennet. On the corner where a road goes left to Sulhampton is *The Spring Inn*, which was originally *The Three Kings*, otherwise known as *Jack's Booth*, a drinking house for the poorer travellers.

The Bath Road sticks to the course of the Kennet all the way to Hungerford. It must have made for an attractive drive for the travellers, and easy going for the horses in good weather, and the traffic on the Kennet and Avon Canal (built 1810) would also be of interest. The canal did take much of the very heaviest goods traffic off the road, making coach travel faster and safer, but this route was prone to frequent flooding and would have been muddy, often forcing coaches to take alternative, higher and more circuitous roads on either bank. It was probably very easy to get lost.

The road now passes the turning to Aldermarston railway station on the left. Aldermarston Wharf has grown up around one of the numerous old wharves along the canal. Immediately after a petrol station on the left stands a building recognisable as an inn, but probably now closed. This was *The Rising Sun*. It had stabling for forty horses and was the booking office for the stage wagons that carried the heavy loads between London and Bath.

Villages that used to perch higher up the slopes with only a scattering of cottages or inns on the highway have now, with less risk of flooding, moved down to the line of the road, leaving 'Upper' versions of themselves stranded above. This is the case with Woolhampton, the next village, where in coaching days only *The Angel* stood on the highway, with a few cottages straggling up the slope towards what is now Upper Woolhampton. *The Angel* has been rebuilt on the same site but the original inn was right up to the road's edge. It was a more significant inn than *The Rising Sun* which we pass on the way into the village, and bizarrely, there were originally two *Angels* in the village, although the *Upper Angel* is now *The Falmouth Arms*, a little further along on the same side.

Thatcham (*52 miles*) was once a small market town which shrank to a straggling village once it lost its coaching trade to the railways. As one drives towards the old centre a tiny chapel stands on the right on the edge of a patch of open space. This medieval chapel was purchased by Lady Frances Winchcombe in 1707 and given to the Blue Coat School which she founded in the village for the benefit of poor children. It has been so vigorously restored that it is difficult to recognise how old it is.

The A4 now skirts the historic High Street to the north – the main inn, *The King's Head*, stands on the left at the junction but in 1819 Egan observed that it was, 'a solitary public house...merely to refresh the waggoner.'

Newbury (*55 miles*) is three miles on from Thatcham, and

now so grown that the original lay-out of the town is lost. Originally Newbury's main street ran north-south, from what is now the Bath Road, down to the river crossing. The straggle of houses and inns where this street – now Broadway – met the east-west road was called Speenhamland.

To agricultural and social historians Speenhamland is best known for the Speenhamland System, a form of poor relief intended to mitigate rural poverty caused by high grain prices. It was created in 1795 after a meeting at *The Pelican* inn by local magistrates who used a means-tested system of wage supplements varying according to the number of children and the price of bread. For example, if bread was 1s 2d a loaf, the wages of a family with two children were topped up to 8s 6d a week. Although William Pitt the Younger attempted to have the system adopted nationally by legislation this failed, but it remained into the 1830s in areas with a high risk of unrest, such as those affected by the Swing Riots.

For anyone travelling along the Bath Road Speenhamland meant *The Pelican* itself, a large and magnificent inn where the charges were so steep that they were immortalised in the rhyme:

The famous inn at Speenhamland,

That stands beneath the hill,

May well be called the Pelican,

From its enormous bill.

Its full name was *The George and Pelican*, but the first part always seems to have been dropped. It has been demolished now, but its curved end has been replicated in the modern building that replaces it on the corner where the Bath Road (London Road) meets Broadway and continues on to become Oxford Street.

Despite its prices *The Pelican* was patronised by royalty, Admiral Lord Nelson and just about anyone of any importance who travelled the Bath Road. It was sold in 1786 and the advertisement boasted that, 'The apartments are exceedingly commodious, the cellars good, and the stables and offices in every respect well adapted to the trade of a capital inn.' It had, for over thirty years, offered 'every convenience and accommodation for travellers of the first rank...'

Because Newbury was almost the half-way point on the journey there were numerous other inns to choose from to break the journey – *The Chequers, The Bear, The Bacon Arms, The Lamb and Flag* and *The King's Arms*, or on the hill above Speenhamland, *The Castle*.

For those who only wanted refreshment, rather than a bed, Egan reports, 'some of the coaches make a short stay here to dine; indeed the short time allowed for this necessary refreshment is so short, that the traveller has scarcely *swallowed* a few mouthfuls, when he is interrupted by the coachman that "*all is ready*" and he must either go without his belly-full, or stand a chance of *choking* himself by *bolting* the remainder of his food, if he means to make any thing like a dinner, in order to accommodate the coachman.'

The old road meets the modern A4 as the road climbs towards the village of Speen, or Church Speen, now absorbed into Newbury. This was at the heart of the indecisive second Battle of Newbury in 1644.

Speen to Beckhampton

A4 to Hungerford, Froxfield then Marlborough. Right at first roundabout (London Road) continue into New Road, Oxford Street and High Street (following Town Centre signs), past the church and right onto the A4. Continue through West Kennet, passing Silbury Hill to roundabout with A361 at Beckhampton.

*

About four miles from the site of *The Pelican* the road passes the turning to the right to Hoe Benham and *The Halfway* inn. No inn shows on the early Ordnance Survey map but half a mile further on (just past Halfway Farm which stands on the right hand side of the road) was a tollgate known as Halfway House and the sixty mile stone. The toll was at the halfway point between London and Bristol and the turnpike trust built an extraordinary Gothic-style castellated structure to mark the fact. It was a very shoddy piece of work, apparently, and although it lasted into the 20th century it has long since vanished.

At Hungerford (*64 miles*) the road leaves Berkshire and crosses the River Kennet into Wiltshire.

Hungerford is set off from the Bath Road – another indication that the route is relatively 'new'. The town lies to the south of the Bath Road along the route to Salisbury with only the ancient *Bear* inn on the Bath Road to welcome the traveller. *The Bear's* claim to fame is as the meeting place on 6th December 1688 of William of Orange and the commissioners sent by James II to attempt to negotiate after William had landed at Brixham. William would not co-operate, James fled and the Glorious Revolution was a *fait accompli.*

Once the Bath Road became a major route, and the Kennet and Avon canal began to flourish, the old town grew in prosperity, more inns operated and it is now an attractive place to visit, with many Georgian buildings.

Egan says that it 'has to boast of one good broad street, a capacious market-house, a neat church and some excellent inns. It is, however, a small town, containing not more than 400 houses... Most of the stage-coaches change horses at Hungerford; and if the traveller should prove thirsty, the *"home-brewed"* of this place is really excellent...'

The railway which, somewhat disconcertingly, crosses the wide High Street on a long bridge, killed both the canal and the coaching trade after its arrival in 1841 and the town never regained its earlier prosperity.

After Hungerford the coachman would probably chill the spines of his passengers with the story of Wild Will Darell, a 16th century owner of Littlecote House (now an hotel) to the north of the road. Lurid tales tell of a blindfolded midwife taken on a midnight journey to an unknown house, a woman in childbed and a masked man hurling the new-born baby onto the fire. True or not, the locals spoke of a Spectral Horseman and a Burning Babe haunting the lanes around the house. It was at Littlecote that the final negotiations over James II's departure were carried out.

Littlecote lies just off the Ramsbury Narrow Way, the ancient line of the road which follows the Kennett through Chilton Foliat, Ramsbury and Mildenhall to Marlborough. As well as being three miles further than the route to its south, it was lower, suffered from flooding and was notoriously stony and difficult.

The more modern, higher, route that the road takes today passes through the picturesque village of Froxfield (*66 miles*) with a large pond and an imposing red brick block of alms houses built in 1686 for fifty widows of clergymen.

After Froxfield the road runs along the northern edge of Savernake Forest, highly picturesque and without many disturbing legends of either ghosts or highwaymen to worry the traveller.

Once out of the Forest the road descends Forest Hill which was a major obstacle in coaching days – steep and with a very poor surface.

The anonymous *A Journey to Bath and Bristol* (1717) mentions this notoriously bad section of road:

'From Hungerford we swift went o'er the Plain,

Too soon we came to the destructive Lane,

O fatal way! Here rocks and craggy Stones

Our Limbs distorted, and unlock't our Bones,

The long worn Axle to the Coach, alack!

Gave here a dismal, unexpected crack.'

The passengers had to get out and continue on foot into Marlborough.

The main street of Marlborough (*74 miles*) is perched on the far bank of the river and the road now, as it always has, turns sharply right across the bridge and up a hill before turning left into the very wide High Street which slopes distinctly from the northern side to the southern. Egan described it as 'a respectable corporate town, containing nearly 500 houses, and about 3000 inhabitants.'

At the far end the road again bends round to the right to bypass the castle mound which, it has recently been discovered, is actually prehistoric in origin. A mansion was built in the castle grounds by Lord Seymour in the 17th century. It later became the residence of the Earl of Hertford, was then sold to the Duke of Northumberland and after years of neglect it was leased out in the mid-18th century and became an inn, *The Castle,* which remained in business until 1843 when it became the core of Marlborough College.

For many years *The Castle* was one of the finest and most famous inns in England. Forty stagecoaches changed horses there daily and it had a brisk business with private carriages and post-chaises. On one occasion the Earl of Chatham was forced by an attack of gout to stay there for two weeks and insisted on the entire staff being dressed in his livery while he was in residence.

Many other well-off travellers, especially during the winter, spent several days at *The Castle*, waiting for good weather to venture out into the howling wilderness of the Wiltshire Downs. During the terrible winter of 1836, when snow across the country at Christmas stopped virtually all traffic, drifts on the Wiltshire Downs were up to 16 feet (almost 5 metres) deep. The Duke of Wellington, *en route* to visit the Duke of Beaufort at Badminton was forced to take refuge at *The Castle* on Boxing Day.

The arrival of the railways killed the business of the inn and the date of the transfer to the College is no coincidence.

After leaving Marlborough the road is immediately on the Downs, passing through Fyfield ('of no interest whatever to the inquisitive traveller' according to Egan) to West Kennet. Here *The White Hart,* 'which stands almost alone, excepting a straggling farm-house or two is famed for selling "a cup of good stingo" [old strong beer]…it is of such high repute, that the farmers and coachmen along the road would think it a positive libel upon their want of *taste* to pass by the White Hart, at West Kennet, without drinking the health of the "*old hostess*" who has long had the merit of producing this wholesome liquid.' (Pierce Egan)

Thus fortified, the traveller could view the prehistoric mystery of Silbury Hill, a major landmark right beside the road, and travel on to Beckhampton, the next change.

Beckhampton to Chippenham

Remain on the A4.

*

Antiquarians must have been thrilled to pass through this landscape, the features of which were generally attributed to the Druids. Stonehenge lies to the south, but the massive stones of Avebury – 'the antique and architectural ruins of a large Druid's temple' (Egan) – are close by and the Ordnance Survey map is littered with 'Large Stones', 'Ancient Earthworks' and tumuli. Many must have got off at Beckhampton and stayed to explore the area. As Egan said, 'If the traveller could alight to view this ruin [Avebury], it would amply repay him for his curiosity.'

When travellers booked their seats for Bath they would have had to decide which route to take, because Beckhampton marks a major division. Some coaches continued on to Calne, Chippenham, Corsham and Box and the others went via Devizes, Melksham and Bathford.

The Calne-Box route, available from the middle of the 18th century, is the one that the most prestigious coaches took and is about two miles shorter. This is the route we will be following in detail.

Another old route branched off the Devizes road, skirted Morgan's Hill and the high ground to the north, passed the village of Heddington and descended into the hamlet of Sandy Lane before going through Lacock to Corsham. It is easiest to find the route today from the Sandy Lane end and directions are included in the Chippenham section.

Beckhampton had two inns. Coming from London we first pass *The Waggon and Horses* on the right. This, the survivor, was the humbler of the two and was referred to by Dickens in the *Pickwick Papers* as being 'about half a quarter of a mile from the end of the Downs.' *The Beckhampton Inn*, the larger, and the main posting-house, stands on the far side of the roundabout with the A361. It was converted into training stables back at the end of the 19th century. The place itself is dismissed by Egan as, 'only conspicuous as a place of refreshment,' but he considers the road onwards is a 'delightful ride'.

The road continues over high downland which rises to the south, crowned with Oldborough Castle, a prehistoric hill fort topped with the thirty eight metre tall Lansdowne Column, erected in 1845.

Until 1792 the Bath Road climbed the flank of this hill by a steep and exposed route which can still just be traced. After Beckhampton there is a layby on the left hand side of the road opposite the 82 mile stone. The old road went up to the left from this point, across the steep flank of the hill and descended to the modern road just before Cherhill. A report in the *Bath Journal* of 12th February 1770 recounts the tale of a rider who was forced by severe weather to take refuge at the Beckhampton inn where he met a party of passengers from 'two of the Bath Machines [stagecoaches] on their way to London.' The wind and the snow had been so severe that they had been unable to go on and, when the passengers got out to try and walk, the coaches were blown over.

The Downs were notoriously dangerous in bad weather and in the terrible winter of 1836 three passengers sitting outside on the stage were found to have died of exposure by the time they reached Chippenham.

Travellers after 1780, as they descended into Cherhill, could have looked back and seen the white horse, carved into the chalk on the orders of Dr Allsop, a doctor from Calne. Egan reports that it 'occasions considerable betting amongst the passengers in the different stage-coaches who daily pass it by' but he does not explain what they were betting on.

Cherhill was the base for the notorious Cherhill Gang of highwaymen, also known as the Naked Highwaymen from their tactic of stripping naked and painting themselves white. This must have been both uncomfortable when riding and decidedly chilly in bad weather! They were probably the gang responsible for robbing the Mail in 1811 and then leaving the unconscious body of an unfortunate drunken labourer, Walter Leader, beside the coach and its mortally wounded driver. Walter was hanged for the crime before proof of his innocence was obtained. The gang itself were finally caught, hanged at Devizes and gibbetted on Cherhill Hill.

Passing Cherhill on the right the road continues down Labour in Vain Hill towards Calne (*87 miles*). Calne once flourished as a cloth-making town, prosperous enough for a branch of the Wilts & Berks Canal to be dug to it in 1810. By the end of the 19th century the cloth trade had completely fallen away and the travellers by coach would have seen the town just before it slid into decline. Egan describes it as having 'an excellent market-house, a large inn, and one tolerable street.' In 1899 Charles G. Harper is less flattering, writing of 'a long, stony street of mean characterless stone houses that leads to the centre of the little town...' where the dock of the canal came right up to the main street.

The King's Arms in the High Street still displays its advertising for the *Hope* coach which, 'Leaves this office every morning except Sundays for Bath and Bristol where it arrives at 11 o'clock in time for the following coaches: Chepstow, Tinterne, Monmouth and Hereford also Taunton and Exeter.'

Children in the town were known for their practice of running alongside coaches turning cartwheels for coppers. Pierce Egan wrote of, 'the girls keeping tight hold of petticoats and tumbling over head and heels with the greatest ease and agility, and on quitting the coach they immediately lay themselves down at the side of the road till another coach appeared and so on until end of day.'

Leaving Calne the road swings round to the west, downhill to the valley of the River Marden and the now-vanished canal and then up Black Dog Hill to what is now New Road. The old road would have turned off to the left just before Black Dog Hill becomes steep and looped round to Bowood House, seat of the Marquess of Lansdowne.

The New Road (clearly the main route by the time of the earliest Ordnance Survey map) descends Red Hill and crosses the Wilts & Berks canal before reaching Chippenham and the River Avon and giving the hard-working horses some relief from hills.

At this point it is possible to make a detour to explore the old road over the downs, mentioned above in the Beckhampton section, by taking the left turning onto the A342 (signposted Devizes) to Sandy Lane. Drive past *The George Inn* and fork left into Back Lane. Follow that past Bell Farm and, just after Gore Farm the lane turns sharply left to Heddington. The Old Bath Road continues straight ahead. The metalling disappears and, although it is possible to follow it right over the Downs in an ordinary car, a 4x4 is preferable, especially if it is at all muddy. It is difficult to believe as you climb that this was once a turnpiked road and it gives a feeling for what the journey must have been like for early coach travellers in this wild and exposed area.

The Bear at Sandy Lane was a very well-known inn, renowned for its food and especially 'Sandy Lane Pudding'.

Princess Caroline dined there in 1746 and met with Beau Nash in 1750, but that was virtually the end for this route. A trustees' meeting in 1755 agreed to abandon it, although it was listed in various guides until 1817.

Continuing on the 'modern' route the traveller reached Chippenham (*92 miles*), a prosperous market town dealing in bacon and cheese, strung out along the road from the east leading to the bridge over the Avon. According to Egan it had 'two or three capacious and good inns, about 800 houses, of antique look…the passenger passes through it without any particular interest.' Immediately the bridge was crossed the road swung sharply left, leaving the town behind. Nowadays the High Street is largely pedestrianised, modern roads carry the Bath route over the river avoiding the town centre and the centre itself has extensive modern building. The old Market Place retains the handsome *Angel*, one of the main coaching inns, and gives an impression of what the old town must have been like.

Chippenham to Bath

Remain on the A4. At the foot of the hill down from Box take the last exit at the roundabout [signposted Batheaston] onto London Road East which becomes High Street and then London Road West. Continue across the roundabout with the A4 onto London Road and continue on the A309 [Walcott Street] into central Bath.

*

After Rowden Hill the route towards Bath is fairly level to the hamlet of Pickwick, now swallowed up by Corsham to the left of the road. Egan, however, complains bitterly that, 'for five miles

197

the road produces very few objects to attract the interest of the traveller, excepting the safety of his seat, from the incessant jolting, in fact, almost jumping, the stage experiences upon this stony road.'

The main route would have gone through Corsham itself until the improvements to the Bath Road, especially to accommodate the Mail coaches, meant that a more direct way was cut bypassing the town. Technically the road passes through Lower Pickwick – Upper and Middle are to the north-west – and it is highly likely that it was from here that Dickens took the name of the *Pickwick Papers*. It is known that he took the coach to Bath in 1835 as a twenty three year old journalist and the first part of the *Papers* was published in March 1836.

Corsham possesses more examples of interesting old buildings from the 16th to the 18th centuries than Calne or Chippenham, probably because of being bypassed by the Bath Road. The quarries at Corsham and Box were the source of the famous Bath stone, the oolitic limestone from which the city is constructed.

After Corsham the road, until 1756, went by way of Chapel Plaister and Kingsdown. To follow that route one should fork left onto the B3109 just after leaving Pickwick and follow it to the crossroads with the A365, turning right onto the minor road signposted Kingsdown. This eventually comes out in Bathford.

By remaining on the 'new' 1756 Mail coach route through Box one crosses the railway line and can see on the left the handsome entrance of the Box Tunnel designed by Isambard

Kingdom Brunel for the Great Western Railway and begun in 1838. It was completed in 1841, sounding the death knell for the coaches that clattered across the new railway bridge.

Egan was very taken with Box (*99 miles*). 'The cleanliness of the houses, which are all made of free (or Bath) stone; a neat little church, built of the same materials, adds to the interest of the scene – the useful farrier's shed – the stocks for the unruly, erected more *in terrorem*, perhaps, than of any material service – the appearance of two small inns, of an inviting character – in short Box is truly compact, and may be viewed as no bad prelude to "great Bath".'

Bath is only four miles ahead as one descends the long hill out of Box. When the road reached the River Avon at Bathford it turned right into Batheaston and followed the river round into Bathwick and the city itself. The coach travellers would have had far more time than the modern motorist to appreciate how Bath clings to the surrounding hills and the steepness of the terrain above the Avon valley.

Egan liked Batheaston (*103 miles*) '...a small town of one tolerable street in length, and the appearance of the town is very neat and clean. In the neighbourhood is Bailbrook-Lodge, a recent establishment for the reception of decayed ladies of respectability and high rank, under the patronage and sanction of her late Majesty...several other gentlemen's seats are contiguous to Batheaston, and the prospects and variety of subjects along the road interest the traveller.

'On descending the hill to Walcot, the traveller is actively

199

engaged with the pleasing appearance which the suburbs of this fashionable city offer to his attention.'

Finally the coaches would have made their way past the 106 mile stone, through the Walcott turnpike (just before the point where The Paragon divides off to the right) and driven along Walcott Street with the river on their left and the ground rising steeply to The Paragon on their right. Then they would arrive at last at the Post Office close to the Abbey, the Roman Baths, the Pump Room, the theatre and the delights of Bath. Porters and chairmen would have been waiting for them to take them off to *The White Hart* or *The York Hotel*, the two principal inns.

Pierce Egan was in no doubt that the *York Hotel* was the best place to stay and he considered it was, 'one of the largest and best inns in the kingdom, out of London. Its accommodations are in the first style of excellence…In the season it overflows with company of the highest rank in life. The dining room is equal, if not superior, to the large room at the Crown and Anchor in London. The suite of rooms correspond and are furnished in the most superb manner.'

The hotel, situated where George Street, Broad Street, Lansdowne Road and the Paragon meet is now merely a Travelodge, so modern guests may not experience quite the ambiance that Egan enjoyed.

Index

Aberford 55, 56

Accidents to coaches 63, 94, 194

Ainsworth, Harrison 40, 137

Alconbury 31-2

Aldermarston Wharf 184

Alnwick 72

Angel of the North 65

Anne, Queen 92

Anstey 137

Asenby 58

Ashdown Forest 147, 148

Askerne 45

Austen, Jane 157, 158

Avebury 192

Avon, River 197, 198

Aycliffe 61

Ayot Green 22

Ayton 75

Baldock 25-6

Banks, Sir Joseph 171

Bapchild 107

Bare knuckle boxing *see* Pugilism

Barham Downs 113

Barnby Moor 43

Barnet *see* Chipping Barnet

Bath 153-4, 199-200

Batheaston 199

Bathford 198

Battles

  Barnet (1471) 17, 18

Dunbar (1650) 77

Erpingham (1470) 36

Gonerby (1642) 39

Newbury (1643/4) 184,187

Prestonpans (1745) 78

Bawtry 43-4

Becket, St Thomas à 81, 94, 100, 139

Beckhampton 192-3

Belford 73

Bell Bar 20

Berwick on Tweed 73-4

Bexley Heath 92-3

Biggleswade 26-8

Birtley 65

Blackfriars Bridge 85

Blackheath 88-90

Blagdon Park 69

Blindley Heath 145

Boroughbridge 57-8

Bothwell, Lord 77

Boughton under Blean 107

Box 199

Bramham 55

Brayton 46

Brentford 170

Bridge 113

Brighton 124, 139-40, 152

Bristol road 153

Brixton 123-4

Brocket Park 21

Bronte, Charlotte & Ann 48

Brotherton 54

Brunel, Isambard K. 182, 199

Buckden 30

Buckland 114

Byng, John Viscount Torrington 7, 22-3, 27-8, 32, 35, 36, 38, 39, 40-1, 42-3, 44-5, 48, 54, 56, 94, 99, 105, 111, 112, 116-118, 177, 182

Byron, Lord 41, 115, 166

Calcot 183

Calne 195-6

Canterbury 81, 110-112, 139
  Archbishop of 124, 128

Caroline, Queen 89-90, 197

Chalk 97

Chaplin, William 17

Charcoal production 126, 128

Charles I 35, 76

Charles II 89, 98, 165

Charlotte, Princess 89

Charlton 90

Chartists 122

Chatham 102-103

Chatham, Earl of 191

Chaucer, Geoffrey 83, 108

Cherhill 194-5

Chester le Street 64-5

Chesterfield canal 42

Cheviot Hills 73

Chippenham 197

Chipping Barnet 17, 18

Chiswick 170

Clapham 140-141

Cliff 150

Coal mining 45, 54, 62, 65, 69, 77

Cockburnspath 75-6

Colnbrook 175

Colne, River 174-5

Colsterworth 37

Corsham 198

Coulsdon 130, 131

Cranford Bridge & Park 173

Crawley 134-5

Crayford 93

Cribb, Tom 37

Croft 59-60

Cromwell, Oliver 39, 76, 128-9

Croxdale 63

Croydon 124, 127-8

Cuckfield 137

Cumberland, Duke of 35, 121

Darlington 58, 60-1

Dartford 94-5

Defoe, Daniel 60, 177

Deptford 86-8

Dickens, Charles 29, 84, 97-8, 166, 193, 198

Dockyards 102

Doncaster 44-5, 51-2

Dover 81, 114-118

Duels 32, 88

Dunbar 76-7

Dunkirk (Kent) 108

Durham 64

Easingwold 49

East Finchley 16

East Grinstead 146-7

East Linton 77

East Retford 42-3

Eaton Socon 29

Edinburgh 78-80

Egan, Pierce 170, 171,173, 187, 189, 193, 195, 197, 199

Eldon, Lord 62, 67-8

Elopements 61-2, 67-8, 73-5, 171

English Civil War 39, 40, 76, 128-9, 168, 184

Entercommon 59

Erasmus, Desidarius 109

Ermine Street 12, 31, 34, 37, 55, 58

Evelyn, John 52, 87-8, 89, 92

Falmer 152

Faversham 107

Ferrybridge 53-4

Ferryhill 62

Felton 71

Fiennes, Celia 100, 101, 105, 110, 113, 117

Finchley Common 18

Flooding 28, 29, 182

Footpads *sa* Highwaymen 14, 15, 88, 126

Forest Row 147

Four Horse Club 169, 174, 178

Fox hunting 35, 37

France 81, 116-117

Froxfield 190

Fruit growing 103, 104, 136

Gad's Hill 97

Gamston 42

Ganwick Corner 19

Gateshead 66

Gatton Park 132

Gatwick Airport 133

General Post Office 14

George III 72, 174

George IV *see* Prince Regent

Ghosts 135, 137, 189

Gibbeted corpses 31, 36, 43, 63, 66, 86, 121-2, 138, 173

Girtford 28

Godmanchester 30-1

Godstone Green 145

Gosforth 69

Glasgow 55, 56, 57

Grantham 38-9

Graveley 25

Gravesend 96-7

Great Casterton 36

Great Gonerby 39-40

Great Ponton 38

Great Smeaton 59

Greenhithe 95-6

Grimaldi, Joseph 14, 15

Haddington 77

Hadley Green 18

Hammersmith 167-8

Hand Cross 135-6

Harbledown 108-109

Harlington Corner 173-4

Harlow Green 66

Harper, Charles G. 7, 45, 47, 50, 53, 60, 66, 68, 72, 75, 93, 99, 106, 113, 165, 195

Harrogate 57

Hatfield & Hatfield House 20

Haywards Heath 137-8

Heathrow Airport 173

Henry III 30, 107, 110

Henry V 84, 100, 105

Henry VIII 13, 30, 77, 88-9, 105

Herschel, William & Caroline 176-7

Heyer, Georgette 24, 25

Hickey, William 91-2

Hick's Hall 12, 13

Highgate 14-16

Highwaymen *sa* Footpads 16, 25, 36, 63, 66, 88, 91, 97-8, 121-2, 126, 163-4, 167, 169, 172-3, 180, 194-5

Holland House 166

Holyhead road

Hop growing 106

Hounslow 171-2

Hounslow Heath 172-3

Hungerford 188-9

Huntingdon 29

Hyde Park 159, 162, 163

Inns *sa* under name of place
  prices 23, 28, 111

Iron working 93

Islington 14

Ivel, River 27, 28

Jackson, 'Gentleman' 130-1, 142

Jacobite Rebellion 77-8, 121

James I & VI 40, 73, 89

James II 169, 188

Jersey, Countess of 170-1

Johnson, Dr Samuel 79, 125

Joppa 78

Kennet, River 182, 184, 188

Kennet & Avon Canal 184, 189

Kennington 121-2

Kensington 164-6

King's Arbour 174

Knaresborough 57

Knightsbridge 158-164

Knottingley & Goole Canal 46

Lamberton 75

Lemsford 21

Lewes 150-1

Linton, Mrs Eliza Lynn 98-9

Littlecote House 189

Little Paxton 29-30

London 13-16, 81-2, 157-8

London Bridge 77, 82, 119, 131

Longford 174

Lowfield Heath 134

Lydden 113-114

McAdam, John 17

Maidenhead 179-80

Maidenhead Thicket 180-1

Malcolm III 73

Mardley Heath 23

Maresfield 149

Markham Moor 42

Marlborough 190-1

Marshalsea Prison 84

Martyrs 13, 95, 151

Mary Queen of Scots 77

Medway 99-100

Merstham 131

Metcalfe, John 58

Methodists 122

Micklefield 54-5

Milestones, iron 148

Milton Regis 104

Mitcham 141-2

Molyneux, Thomas 37

More, Sir Thomas 110

Morpeth 70

Murders 31, 43, 49-50, 63, 97-8, 173, 175

Musselburgh 78

Napoleonic Wars 34, 92, 116-117

Nash, Beau 197

Nelson, Horatio 71, 118, 135, 141, 187

Newark 40-1

Newbury 185-7

Newcastle upon Tyne 65, 66-9

Newchapel 145-6

New Cross 86

Newington 103-104

New River Head 14

Norbury 126

Norman Cross prison camp 34

Northallerton 51, 58

North Finchley 16

Northfleet 96

Northumberland, Duke of 72, 170

North York Moors 50

Nutley 148

Old North Road 12, 31

Ordnance Survey baseline 174

Ospringe 107

Osterley Park 170

Paine, Thomas 150-1

Paper mills 30, 42, 105, 114

Patcham 139

Pease Pottage 135

Pepys, Samuel 31, 88

Peter the Great 87-8

Pickwick 197-8

Pilgrims 81, 83, 94, 109, 114, 139

Pity Me 54-5

Portobello 78

Potter's Bar 19

Povey Cross 133

Prince Regent 44, 131, 135, 143

Pugilism 37, 122, 130-1, 135

Pumps for dust-laying 174, 182-3

Purley 130

Pyecombe 139

Quarries 90, 95, 131

Racecourses 35, 44, 60, 69, 142-3, 152

Railways 6, 19, 30, 60-1, 182, 198-9

  horse-drawn 60-1, 129, 141-2

Rainham 103

Ramsbury Narrow Way 189-90

Reading 181-2

Redhill 133

Reigate 133, 143-4

Rennie, John 77

Repton, Humphrey 28, 152

Ripon 57

Road builders 17, 58, 70

Robin Hood's Well 52-3

Rochester 100-102

Rosher, Jermiah 96

Roman remains 34, 57, 67, 81

Roman roads 12, 34, 37, 55, 58, 81, 95, 123, 145

Rowlandson, Thomas 134-5, 137

Rusheyford 62

St Neots 29

Salt Hill 169, 178

Sandy Lane 196-7

Savernake Forest 190

Sawtry 32

Scarthing Moor 41

Scotland 74-80

Scott, John see Eldon, Lord

Scott, Sir Walter 39-40, 41, 53, 78, 166

Scrooby 43

Selby 46-7

Severndroog Castle 91

Shelley, Percy B 48

Shooters Hill 90-2

Sittingbourne 104-106

Slough 175-8

Smithfield 13

Smitham Bottom 130-1, 144

Smuggling 78, 136, 138, 139, 149

Snow as hazard 138, 191, 194

Southwark 82-5, 119-20

Spas & mineral springs 14, 45, 59-60, 92, 124-5

Speenhamland 186-7

Stagecoach business, The 16, 17, 30, 106-6, 155-6

Stamford 35-6

Stanborough 21

Stanmer Park 152

Staplefield Common 136

Stephenson, Robert 67

Stevenage 24-5

Stilton 33

Stockwell 123, 140

Stone 95

Stone Pound 138

Streatham 123, 124-6

Strood 99

Sunderland Bridge 63-4

Sutton 142

Swarland Park 71

Syon Park 170

Tangier Wood 143

Tees, River 59, 60

Telford, Thomas 17, 70

Temple Ewell 114

Tempsford 28

Thatcham 185

Theale 183-4

Thinford 63

Thirsk 50

Thornton Heath 126-7

Thornton le Street 50-1

Thrale, Mrs Hester 125

Tooke, John Horne 130

Tooting 141

Topcliffe 58

Torrington, Viscount *see* Byng, John

Tranent 78

Travellers, refreshments & accommodation for 23, 27-8 32, 33, 37, 43, 79, 96, 136, 143, 150, 187, 196-7 *sa* Byng, John

Trent, River 40, 41

Turner, J.M.W. 70, 72

Turnham Green 168

Turnpike trusts 17, 47, 94, 148, 151-2, 154

Turpin, Dick 16, 40, 91, 98, 127

Tuxford 41-2

Tweed, River 73-4

Tweedmouth 73

Twining, Rev. Thomas 39, 43

Twyford 181

Tyne, River 65

Uckfield 149

Vauxhall Bridge 121, 123

Verrall, William 150

Wainewright, Thomas Griffiths 168

Walpole, Horace 169

Walshford 57

Wandle, River 128, 129

Wansford 34-5

Waterloo churches 122

Watling Street 81, 95, 112

Wear, River 62, 63, 64, 65

Welling 92

Wellington, Duke of 158, 191

Wellesley, Marquis 158, 163

Welwyn 22-3

Wentbridge 53

Wesley, Charles & John 122

Westbourne, River 159

West Kennet 192

Westminster Bridge 120

West Thurston 71

Wetherby 55-6

Whetstone 17

Whittington, Dick 15

Wilberforce, William 141, 164

Wilkes, John 164

William III 169, 188

William IV 116

Wilts & Berks Canal 195, 196

Windmills 29, 42

Woolhampton 184

Woolwich 90

Wyatt, James 147

Wych Cross 148

York 47-9

About the Author

Louise Allen writes historical romance, time-slip romantic mystery, historical mystery romance and the occasional historical non-fiction book. She lives on the North Norfolk coast close to the 18th century seaside town of Cromer. She is a passionate collector of late Georgian and Regency ephemera and prints and is the author of over seventy books, mainly set in the Georgian and Regency period. She also blogs about Georgian life at https://janeaustenslondon.com/

Twitter: LouiseRegency

Full details of all her books, including extracts and buy-links, can be found at www.louiseallenregency.com

Printed in Great Britain
by Amazon

59374615R00116